The Persistence of Tragedy:

Episodes in the History of Drama

The Persistence of Tragedy: Episodes in the History of Drama

by John L. Mahoney

Professor of English, Boston College

Lectures Delivered for
The National Endowment for the Humanities

Boston Public Library
Learning Library Program

Boston, Trustees of the Public Library
of the City of Boston, 1985

Library of Congress Cataloging in Publication Data

Mahoney, John L.
   The persistence of tragedy.
   "Lectures delivered for the National Endowment for
the Humanities, Boston Public Library, Learning
Library Program."
     Bibliography: p. 125
     1. Tragedy. I. Boston Public Library. National
Endowment for the Humanities Learning Library Program.
II. Title.
PN1892.M323 1985   809.2'512   84-23947
ISBN 0-89073-101-2

Photographic Credits

p. 22, The theater of Dionysus. Patricia Mahoney photograph, 1984.

p. 32, The theater of Epidaurus. Nancy Donovan photograph, 1984.

p. 44, Richard Burton as Hamlet. Harvard Theatre Collection.

p. 54, Paul Schofield as King Lear. Harvard Theatre Collection.

p. 85, The haunted Tyrone family. Harvard Theatre Collection.

p. 97, Thomas Mitchell as Willy Loman. Harvard Theatre Collection.

p. 119, Henderson Forsythe as Vladamir. © Alix Jeffry, Harvard Theatre Collection.

For Ann, as always

Contents

Preface

WHEN Philip McNiff, the distinguished Librarian Emeritus of the Boston Public Library, first called me about the possibility of lecturing in the National Endowment for the Humanities Learning Library program, I was both honored and challenged by the invitation. I was honored because of the prestige of the program and its previous lecturers, and challenged by the possible topics for a relatively short series of six lectures. Mr. McNiff's general suggestions revolved around drama, and the prospect of talking with bright and eager audiences about that genre was a happy one. At the same time the prospect of sweeping surveys of names and dates, of summarizing hordes of plots, of trying to cover historical periods was not a happy one for me, nor was it, I felt, for those audiences.

And so while delighted with the idea of lecturing on drama, I resolved to narrow my focus. I had taught and written on drama during my college and university teaching over the years, had taught individual dramatists like Shakespeare, Ibsen, O'Neill, Williams, Miller, and others. I have always been an incurable theatergoer, following the New York and Boston stage as well as the venturesome regional productions of groups like the American Repertory Company of Harvard University, the Huntington Theater Company of Boston, and the Trinity Square Playhouse of Providence, Rhode Island.

As I thought especially about my teaching, I remembered several stimulating and rewarding seminars in "Tragedy," seminars in which, with the kind of intelligent and enthusiastic graduate and undergraduate students I have enjoyed teaching at Boston College over the years, we explored the plays of the

Greeks—Aeschylus, Sophocles, Euripides; of the great Elizabethan Shakespeare; of early modern European dramatists like Ibsen, Strindberg, Shaw; of the peculiarly Irish genius of Synge, O'Casey and others; of modern American and European dramatists like O'Neill, Williams, Miller, Albee, Macleish, Beckett, and many others. The tragic impulse in literature, in drama especially, has fascinated teachers, critics, and students from the beginning. The spectacle of a good man or woman suffering unjustly and yet enduring, challenging, at times perishing in the struggle has captured the attention and imagination of the greatest writers.

With memories of those seminars, I resolved that I would lecture on the persistence of tragedy in world drama and that I would—knowing that any attempt at comprehensiveness would be futile—focus on key episodes in the history of the genre and particularly on major figures and plays within each episode. Yes, many favorites of my audiences would be neglected, but there would be the satisfaction of knowing that my choices— Sophocles, Shakespeare, Ibsen, O'Neill, Miller, Williams, and Beckett—would be adequate to carry the burden of a great tradition. And there would be the further satisfaction of knowing that plays like *Antigone, Oedipus the King, Hamlet, King Lear, A Doll's House, Hedda Gabler, The Iceman Cometh, Long Day's Journey into Night, Death of a Salesman, The Glass Menagerie, A Streetcar Named Desire,* and *Waiting for Godot* could carry the same burden.

Such is the background of these modest attempts to deal with the recurring pattern of tragedy in Western literature and with our continuing interest in it even today in our so-called tragic age. Professors Albert M. Folkard and P. Albert Duhamel first introduced me to the special pleasures of tragedy a good many years ago, especially in their classes on Shakespeare and literary criticism. Elliot Norton, recently retired Dean of American theater critics, was my colleague at Boston College for many years, and I profited greatly from many conversations with him, but chiefly from his regular critical writings in a number of Boston newspapers over the years and from his enormously popular Public Television program *Elliot Norton Reviews* on WGBH, Channel Two in Boston. His wise reflections and infectious enthusiasm, still alive and well during these years of a happy retirement, represent the highest standards of dramatic criticism.

No one, however, has had a greater influence on my thinking and on these lectures than my former student, Professor Stephen Fix of Williams College, whose searching questions and provocative ideas enlivened one of those memorable courses mentioned above. His unpublished Scholar of the College Thesis on "The Phenomenology of Tragedy"—which I had the pleasure of co-directing some ten years ago when he was a Boston College senior—reflects many engaging conversations we had during the time he was writing. He, I hope, will recognize in these lectures his keen philosophical sense, his command of the historical roots of tragedy, his masterful ability to read drama and at the same time to see it as something only fully revealed in performance. I owe him a great debt.

Worth Douglas and Barbara Berger of the Brighton Branch of the Boston Public Library, the handsome new building where these lectures were delivered, extended warm hospitality and professional support that made my Thursday evening visits a pleasure. Their encouragement and enthusiasm are largely responsible for the publication of the lectures. Liam Kelly, Acting Director of the Boston Public Library, and Jane Manthorne, Assistant to the Director, saw to it that the spoken word became the printed word. The handsome format of this book is the work of Richard Zonghi, Chief of Graphic Services. Patricia A. Mahoney has provided once again superior advice on matters of design; and she, along with Nancy Donovan, is responsible for several splendid photographs of Greek theaters. I'm grateful as always for special talents. Special thanks are due to my Department Chairman Dennis Taylor for support of all kinds in the preparation of the manuscript and to Carol Fisher for a masterful typing job.

For love, encouragement, and support as always, my thanks to my wife Ann, and to John Jr., Lenor, Pat, and Bill. For never-failing friendship and for the gifts of their glorious music, I again offer thanks to Jackie and Roy Kral and to Harry Locke. They attended the lectures and, like Coleridge's Wedding Guest, could not choose but hear.

11

Introduction:
Backgrounds of Tragedy

I N some ways these lectures can be seen as narrow, restrictive, even arrogant, for I have chosen to rule out quite arbitrarily a whole range of literary genres in order to pursue the persistence of tragedy in drama only. I can, of course, plead that the sponsors of this series invited me to speak on drama, and to take some approach with which I would feel comfortable. I can further plead that the restriction of time set by six lectures is good reason for neglecting the novel and other literary forms even though these forms contain elements that I associate with tragedy.

Yet neither of these pleas would adequately explain my decision to focus on drama as the vehicle for discussing the persistence of the tragic vision in Western literature. In the fiction of Hawthorne, Melville, Dostoyevsky, Tolstoy, Flaubert, and so many others, the characters, conflicts, and disasters that fill the great dramas are certainly apparent. And yet it is in drama that the fullness of the tragic seems most vividly revealed. Drama, as our first literary handbooks teach us, is action, not narration, not lyric expression. Drama shows us human beings caught in a variety of situations, and in the process responding to those situations, interacting with one another, winning or losing, laughing or crying. Yes, there are these dramatic elements in the great novels, in the best lyric poems, but these elements almost always seem subservient to the larger responsibilities of telling a story, giving vent to personal feeling, capturing a mood.

As we sit in the theater, however, we become witnesses to the actions of men and women—physical actions or psychological struggles—to the dilemna of Antigone as she chooses love of family over devotion to human law, to the response of Hamlet to the challenge of his father's ghost, to the fierce struggle of Nora Helmer to escape the claustrophobic world of her husband Torvald, to the romantic but destructive dreams of a Blanche Dubois or a Willy Loman, to the sad-happy clinging to each other of Vladamir and Estragon in that barren landscape of *Waiting for Godot*. And, of course, in tragic drama the intensity of action is all the greater—taut, tense, exciting, exhilarating, frightening. The issues that confront the characters—the call of conscience, the demands of justice, the need to survive—are so much issues of life and death, so large and so compelling that their enactment in the darkness of a theater involves us so intimately, so powerfully that we often feel drawn out of our seats and onto the stage. We would almost play a special role of our own, siding now with this character, now with that one, urging this character to shout more loudly for the rightness of his course and that character to demand more fully her need to be recognized and heard. Many will understandably be quick to say that they feel the same closeness to the characters of stories or poems, but for the present writer there is no greater assault on the imagination and emotions than in the performance of superior actors in a drama of consequence.

But what of the persistence of what is called tragedy in very different cultures and in very different dramatic configurations? What of the wide variation of critical opinion on the meaning of the term itself? Has a single ideal of tragedy continued across cultures and across the centuries, or has the ideal perished and the term become hopelessly confused as we use it today? The answers to such questions will vary alarmingly, but those questions will not go away. Many of us leave a production of *Death of a Salesman* today and discuss it as if it were part of a grand tradition, as if it shared a kinship with *Oedipus the King*. Others leave a production of *Waiting for Godot* bemoaning the loss of the heroic ideal, of great men and women meeting suffering and disaster with courage. These lectures will not attempt any definitive answers or solutions; such would be the height of vanity. But they will pursue the questions, examine the persistence of plays called tragedies, and at least wonder about the possibilities of the term as a way of discussing plays that are seemingly very different in substance and form.

Plays called tragedies take us back to ancient Athens and forward to 1984. The Broadway stage over the last few years has seen superior revivals of the *Medea* of Euripides—with Judith Anderson and Zoe Caldwell—and of Millier's *Death of a Salesman*—with Dustin Hoffman as Willy Loman, and both plays have been hailed for their tragic quality. And the term has fascinated literary theorists as early as Aristotle and as recently as Arthur Miller with each critic speaking confidently about certainly essential ingredients—the nature of the tragic world, the characteristics of its heroes and heroines, the roots of their suffering and loss, the impact of their downfalls on audiences. Aristotle in his *Poetics*, with a keen sense of the many tragedies of Aeschylus, Sophocles, and Euripides he had witnessed, speaks of the hero of great magnitude laid low by a tragic flaw and evoking feelings of pity and fear which ultimately undergo some kind of purgation in the audience.

Chaucer's Monk in *The Canterbury Tales* captures a peculiarly medieval tinge which emphasizes the impact of fortune in human life, a fortune that transcends individual responsibility to make men and women the playthings of a mysterious, even fickle force.

> Tragedie is to seyn a certeyn storie,
> As olde bokes maken us memorie,
> Of him that stood in greet prosperitee
> And is y-fallen out of heigh degree
> Into miserie, and endeth wrecchedly.

Whether the spectacle is of evil creatures—Lucifer, Adam, Balthasar, Nero—or of the virtuous—Samson, Zenobia, Peter of Cyprus, Count Ugolino, Alexander the Great—Alexander's cry seems to capture the Monk's, and for that matter a good part of the medieval charge against the fickleness of fate: "Alas! who shall helpe to endyte/False fortune, and poison to despyse,/The which two of al this wo I wyte?"

There are also, of course, the great English Renaissance tragedies of Thomas Kyd and Christopher Marlowe, portraits of overwhelmingly large figures, in some ways embodiments of evil who meet disaster as a kind of poetic justice—Tamburlaine, Faustus. And then, of course, there is the major figure of the age,

15

William Shakespeare, a dramatist of enormous versatility and yet one whose tragedies seem to tower above the comedies and history plays among his works. Many critics have been quick to see something of the Aristotelian ideal in *Hamlet, King Lear, Othello, Macbeth* and other tragedies, the great figure meeting his downfall grandly in a world where fate still plays its role. Yet there are new strains, a greater emphasis on a certain freedom of choice in the characters, a "vicious mole" in nature, to borrow Hamlet's phrase, which upsets the balance of both microcosm and macrocosm, which brings struggle, disaster, even death, and yet which culminates in some mysterious quiet after conflict, some restoration, however faint, of order after chaos, some sense of meaning emerging from great pain and suffering.

It is in the nineteenth century that critics and literary historians note the sharpest break from the tradition of tragedy, a break that moves the arena of tragic drama from the court to the living room, from the battlefield to the backyard, from the chariot to the streetcar. The new tragedy—we see already the dangers involved in using the term too categorically—is, of course, not something that exists in isolation from the social situation in which it is written, produced and performed. Indeed that very social situation is seen by many critics to be the villain of the piece. They view the collapse of the French Revolution, the reactionary post-Revolution settlements, the full flowering of the Industrial Revolution as undermining the earlier ideals of tragic magnitude, of heroism on a large scale, of great men and women whose flaws shook entire societies. What emerged was a much more constricted world of ordinary people struggling either with the society or with themselves to reach some kind of self-realization, some kind of personal freedom and happiness. Henrik Ibsen is certainly a leader in a drama that responds to that world in its manner, settings, characters, and problems. Ibsen brought to the stage in Nora Helmer, Hedda Gabler, Mrs. Alving, and others men and women who may lack grandeur, but who are willing to fight for individual freedom even when the fight brings suffering and death.

Nowhere is the impact of the new realism, the new egalitarianism, the new social-psychological tragedy more closely viewed and more carefully studied than in twentieth-century

America—in Eugene O'Neill, Arthur Miller, Tennessee Williams, to name just a few. Here the characters seem even smaller. No family curse, no large looming power of fate, no Christian idea of sin fully explains the plight of the doomed Tyrone family, of Willy Loman, of the dreaming Wingfields, of Blanche Dubois. So often characters and families seem trapped by the past, by illusions. While the struggle is still there, it seems so much less spectacular than that of an Oedipus or Lear or even Nora Helmer. And yet critics argue strongly that, though we seem in the presence of lesser mortals, we see in these creatures something of ourselves, something that links them with even the greatest classical heroes and heroines.

Arthur Miller's celebrated essay, "Tragedy and the Common Man" in *The New York Times* of February 27, 1949 has become the *Poetics* of modern drama, and we shall return to it later. For Miller, ". . . the tragic feeling is evoked in us when we are in the presence of a character who is ready to lay down his life, if need be, to secure one thing—his sense of personal dignity." Defending the common man as tragic hero, he argues: "From Orestes to Hamlet, Medea to Macbeth, the underlying struggle is that of the individual attempting to gain his 'rightful' place in society."

Beyond even the bleakest of O'Neill or Williams or Miller is the large phenomenon of very recent drama, especially the plays of Samuel Beckett, and with his *Waiting for Godot* the problem of these lectures becomes most acute. Vladamir and Estragon, two clownish heroes or perhaps anti-heroes, stand on a stark, ravaged landscape. They are alone, passing the time, proposing the possibility of suicide. They are waiting for Godot—whoever he is—who never comes, enduring and finding meaning only in that capacity for endurance and in the possibilities of tenderness and love. Beckett's vision—called now tragic, now tragicomic—forces us to examine our questions more deeply.

The title of our lectures is "The Persistence of Tragedy," and therein lies the implication of some magic formula or definition held in advance by the lecturer and ready to be applied neatly to any play. Such, I hope, is not the case. Yet while entering this disclaimer, the lecturer must be candid in sharing a need to explore the idea that, in spite of enormous diversity and variety

17

—fifth-century B.C. Athens; Elizabethan England; nineteenth-century Europe; twentieth-century Europe and America; Oedipus the King; Hamlet, Prince of Denmark; Nora Helmer, bank-manager's wife; Willy Loman, New England salesman—there are certain basic similarities that may make it possible to see a continuity of concern. We are, it seems, drawn to the plight of the basically good man or woman who—because of some human frailty or error of judgment or perhaps without apparent cause—suffers, even dies. Such a fate prompts this man or woman to question, to challenge, and often as a result to bring down a family, a kingdom, to disturb a universe. Yet from viewing the tragedy we feel neither despair nor easy optimism. There is rather a sense of calm after a violent storm, or an order restored to the human organism after a threatening cancer has been removed, even the simple peace that follows a battle. At times the affirmation may be strong; the order may be clear. At others the suffering and violence may shake us, may test even our will to believe, to go on, but, in Keats's phrase, through a special magic of the work "all disagreeables evaporate." Almost always is the sense that we spectators are watching embodiments of ourselves coming to terms with the possibilities and limits of mortality, and in so doing we become richer and wiser and more fully human.

The following lectures will, of course, savor the delight of tragedy from the Greeks to the present, not necessarily to superimpose these observations on a variety of plays, but rather to test them for better or for worse, to see to what extent they illuminate and enrich our discussion of the plays. The play's the thing in these lectures, so if we have questions to ask, we have the beauty of the drama to wonder about and to admire.

CHAPTER 1

Sophocles and Greek Tragedy

"Wisdom is the supreme part of happiness; and
reverence towards the gods must be inviolate.
Great words of prideful men are ever punished
with great blows, and, in old age, teach the
chastened to be wise."

Sophocles, *Antigone*

SINCE tragedy is no recent literary development, the reader
or viewer who would understand and enjoy it must come to
terms with its remote and somewhat misty origins. There is no
more misguided pedagogical or popular discussion than one in
which the participants view the awful dilemma of an Oedipus as
if he were a twentieth-century American or the response of a
Hamlet to the death of his father or the decision of a Nora
Helmer or the dream of a Willy Loman or the waiting for Godot
of Vladamir and Estragon as if these characters were being
presented in the theater of the Acropolis in fifth-century B.C.
Athens. This is not to say that great plays do not achieve their
enduring values and pleasures by cutting across the ages or that
they can be understood only against the backdrop of the eras in
which they were written and performed. It is, however, to
underline the importance of seeing the dramatic genius of the
artist in some connection with the cultural milieu in which he
wrote.

The reader of Aeschylus, Sophocles, and Euripides—generally
cited as the major figures of Greek tragedy—should perhaps
recall the ancient world of ninth and tenth-century B.C. Greece
with its aristocratic ideals, its larger than life heroes and
heroines, its god-drenched atmosphere with divinities touching
every aspect of life with their power. It is the world of the *Iliad*
and the *Odyssey*, of the abduction of Helen of Troy by Paris of
Greece and the great Trojan War that ensued. It is a world

whose characters embody a certain largeness of mind and of spirit, a standard of perfection in act and deed. Plato, as did Sir Philip Sidney centuries later, saw Homer as a great artist, but chiefly as a teacher, a teacher of the tragic poets, and the *Iliad* and the *Odyssey* as epic portrayals of humankind as it ought to be. Aristotle saw the educative side of the art more broadly as a *psychogogia*, a leading out of the spirit to know and feel and embody ideals of virtue and grace.

This ideal remained for centuries as just that, an ideal, not a formal structure. It remained for it to be absorbed by a nation, to be enacted in a larger societal context. As Werner Jaeger puts it, "Culture is simply the aristocratic ideal of a nation, increasingly intellectualized."[1] Athens was that political entity, that city-state—small though it was—that ultimately embodied the ideal in the fifth century B.C. Balancing the Spartan ideal of the state with the Ionian emphasis on the individual, little Athens seemed to develop and reach a point of perfection, on the one hand achieving political strength and on the other a concern with ideals of justice, humaneness, and beauty, with art and the artists. There was a certain celebration of life, of the mind in action, of the power of man. Edith Hamilton captures this spirit superbly as she compares Greek life-centeredness with Eastern spiritualism:

> The Hindoo artist was subject to no conditions; of all artists he was the freest. The Egyptian was submissive to the ways of nature and the dogmas of the priest; the Greek was limited by his mind that would not let him lose sight of the things that are seen; the Hindoo was unhampered by anything outside of himself except the materials he worked in and even there he refused to recognize a limitation. The art of India and of all the nations of the East she influenced shows again and again sculpture that struggles to be free of the marble. No artists have ever made bronze and stone move as these did. There was nothing fixed and rigid for them; nothing in the world of spirit is fixed and rigid. Hindoo art is the result of unchecked spiritual force, a flood held back by no restraints.[2]

Athens, at the height of its material and cultural prosperity, felt an even stronger sense of self, of national consciousness as it turned back the superior attacking forces of Persia. At this special moment of power and pride, philosophers and artists sought to come to terms with central and complex questions. It was a movement from myth to rational inquiry which brought such questions as: What is man? What is his relationship to the gods? What is justice? Why do men suffer, and does the suffering have any meaning? And in the midst of this spirit of inquiry Athens produced a remarkable body of dramatic literature, the work largely of Aeschylus (c. 525-455 B.C.), Sophocles (c. 496-405 B.C.), and Euripides (480-406 B.C.).

The roots of this surge of great tragic drama are difficult to trace although there is a certain general agreement as to the probable sources. There is that most primitive source in the rituals of worship of the god Dionysus, the dance and song of the community to gain fertility. From primitive, unformed celebrations more formal rituals developed until Pisistratus, a late sixth-century B.C. Athenian ruler, established a formal festival and state holiday in 534 B.C. Development proceeded rapidly. It was at one of these festivals that one Thespis (a name we now popularly associate with actors—Thespian) emerged from the larger group to play the role of the god, reciting verses to the chorus which sang the ancient dithyrambs or hymns. A kind of synthesis emerged from these beginnings—a combination of song, dance, and now the first, albeit primitive, signs of action, dialogue, conflict. We actually know very little of the actual workings of drama at this time. It is only in the fifth-century that we see drama, and specifically tragedy, take on sharp characteristics. Using the ancient myths of Prometheus, Medea, Oedipus, and many others, tragedy took on a religious and humanistic function. Dramatists framed artistically the special conflicts inherent in the myths, and the lyric slowly gave way to the dramatic, to the themes embodied in Prometheus' struggle with Zeus, Oedipus' search for himself, Medea's fierce murder of her husband and children.

The tradition of festivals became more firmly established with competitions held during the spring religious holidays known as the Dionysia. We have a fair idea of the nature of those holidays and of the dramatic competitions. Plays were presented in groups of four, three tragedies and a satyr or comic play. Three

The theater of Dionysus, on the south slope of the Acropolis in Athens, where many of the great Greek plays were performed.

dramatists were chosen for a given day, and a jury of citizens awarded prizes.

The most celebrated theater was cut out of the rock at the southeast end of the Acropolis in a roughly semicircular segment of 215º. It was 350 feet across, 250 feet deep, open to the elements, with a hundred rows of seats for spectators. With the simplest of sets and costuming, with actors wearing masks, elevated shoes and padded dress to give a sense of largeness, the focus was clearly on the action. The structure of the tragedies combined music, dance, and drama. A prologue set forth the basic exposition, was followed by alternating choral odes and acted scenes, and concluded with a denouement. With the audience already in command of the basic myth, a premium was placed on the artistry of the dramatist, on his ability to handle recognitions, reversals, irony, and other techniques. Tragic drama had reached a remarkable stage of development in fifth-century Athens; some would say it has never been equalled. It is to that tragedy, and to one of its premier examples, that we now turn our attention.

Aeschylus is traditionally—and perhaps quite rightly—called the father of Greek tragedy. An innovator of sorts, he brought the drama from rather primitive ritual to a genuine sense of theater. It was he who introduced a second actor, gave greater importance to the dramatic encounter of dialogue, developed masks, some primitive costuming, and scenic accessories. He had known the greatness of Athens, had fought at the decisive battles at Marathon and Salamis, had known the great triumph over Persia and the national pride that came with it. How often he was drawn to the sense of a flaw in the universe, to the problem of pain and suffering, to the image of men and women as sinners, violators.

Aeschylus is clearly the religious dramatist. For him there is a Divine Law which gives meaning to existence even when that law angers and bewilders, a Supreme Power that is greater than even the lesser gods of mythology. His God is a quick, retributive, direct force which punishes sinners even as those sinners—often caught by fate—evoke our sympathy. Where then, we say, is the attraction, where the hope in the ancient but futile struggle of Prometheus with Zeus, the bloodstained legends of the House of Atreus? Prometheus is both sinner and yet champion, stealing the divine fire to bring light to mankind and yet challenging the established order. The doom of Clytemnestra and Agamemnon and Orestes in the *Oresteia* trilogy is rooted in primitive family curses, and yet in these plays we see characters meeting disaster grandly, being purged through suffering. His is a drama filled with religious axioms: *"Whosoe'er shall take the sword/Shall perish by the sword"*; "While Time shall be, while Zeus in heaven is lord,/His law is fixed and stern;/On him that wrought shall vengeance be outpoured-/The tides of doom return"; "The blow that fells the sinner is of God"; "Tis Zeus alone who shows the perfect way/Of knowledge: He hath ruled,/Men shall learn wisdom, by affliction schooled."

Aeschylus' is a relatively simple drama in structure, tableau-like, focusing on one great action. His characters are creatures with one dominant trait—the courage and daring of Prometheus, the ferocity of Clytemnestra. With a poetry of rich

23

language and imagery, he launches Greek tragedy, dramatizing a deep faith that the fullest wisdom is gained through suffering. No passage better captures his ultimate vision than the closing of the *Eumenides,* the third play of the Oresteia trilogy. Condemned to revenge his father Agamemnon's death by killing his mother Clytemnestra, Orestes is hunted and haunted by the Furies. These Furies, however, are ultimately transformed into friendly forces and finally, as Orestes faces his jury at the trial, Justice is softened by Mercy, and the decisive vote for acquittal is cast by Athena. H.D.F. Kitto captures the scene nicely:

> So, in the tremendous finale of this trilogy, the Athenian people saw, in dramatic symbolism, the age-long growth of religion and society brought to its fulfilment among themselves, as, persuaded by the goddess of the city, the last rebels against Zeus accept their new home in Athens, and pass out of the theater, no longer Furies but Kindly Ones, to be led in imaginary procession from the southern to the northern face of the sacred rock."[3]

If Aeschylus is the most conservative of the Greek tragedians, Euripides must rank as the most radical, the most iconoclastic. One senses in his plays—and he wrote some 75 including *Alcestis, Medea, Hecuba, The Trojan Women*—more skepticism about prevailing orthodoxies, about the possibility of certitude, the glory of man, the glamor of war, the nobility of suffering. He frequently debunks the gods, pities those men and women who suffer unjustly, realistically portrays the tragic situation of humankind. The influence of the skeptical Sophists can be felt in his works, and his plays—although they won only five first prizes at the festival competitions—appealed greatly to the social and philosophical radicals. Aristotle, in his famous evaluation of the three major tragedians in the *Poetics,* says that Euripides portrayed men as they are.

Euripides was, of course, a late fifth-century figure, and had seen the decline of the once strong Athenian empire, the criticism of democracy, the erosion of traditional religion, the rise of free thought. Above all, he felt the impact of the Peloponnesian War between Athens and Sparta as it weakened the spiritual and material fiber of Athens. He could not rationalize injustice and human suffering, but chose to admire the goodness in humankind and to pity the suffering of men and women in an apparently unreasonable world. Hence his heroes and heroines often seem less Aristotelian, less grand, not so much guilty sinners as victims of a destructive element in humanity. There is a rambling structure in his plays and no great probing of complex characters, but there is a central unity of tone, a sense of the plight of men and women caught in the trap of life. His are powerful if single-minded characters. We remember Medea's tremendous love for her husband Jason, a love that moved her to attempt everything—the killing of a brother, the deceiving of a father—in Jason's quest for the Golden Fleece of Colchis, and we likewise remember how that love turns to savage hatred as she takes revenge on the infidelity of Jason by killing him and their children. In a play filled with reverberations for the modern reader, Euripides' increasing disillusionment with Athenian culture and politics culminates with Athens' savage invasion of the tiny island of Melos and the punishment of its citizens for their policy of neutralism. *The Trojan Women*—certainly one of the great anti-war plays—may not be as elaborately crafted, but it has that unity of tone spoken of earlier, a brilliance of language, a powerful intensity that contrasts the pride of the conquerors and the pathetic suffering of the conquered. There are few more striking portraits of the victims of war than the venerable Hecuba, the brave Andromache, the pathetic Cassandra, the bewildered Astyanax, not creatures with tragic flaws, but tragic sufferers who endure and who gain a kind of greatness by the endurance. Hecuba's speech towards the end of the play captures vividly so much of the Euripidean tragic spirit:

> Lo, I have seen the open hand of God!
> And in it nothing, nothing save the rod
> Of mine affliction, and the eternal hate,
> Beyond all lands, chosen and lifted great
> For Troy! Vain, vain were prayer and incense-swell
> And bulls' blood on the altars! . . . All is well.
> Had He not turned us in His hand, and thrust
> Our high things low and shook our hills as dust,
> We had not been this splendour, and our wrong
> An everlasting music for the song
> Of earth and heaven![4]

Sophocles, the focus on this lecture on Greek tragedy, was, it seems, the favorite tragedian of Aristotle, and *Oedipus the King* the perfect example of his idea of tragedy considered earlier. We might linger over that definition a bit at this point. Tragedy for Aristotle in the *Poetics* is no mere drama of catastrophe. It is a thing of art, "an imitation of an action that is complete, and whole, and of a certain magnitude." Its hero or heroine can be no ordinary mortal destroyed by mere accident or rank depravity. The great tragedy "should, moreover, imitate actions which excite pity and fear, this being the distinctive mark of tragic imitation." The ideal is neither the completely virtuous nor completely vicious person, but "the character between these two extremes,—that of a man who is not eminently good and just, yet whose misfortune is brought about not by vice or depravity, but by some error or frailty. He must be one who is highly renowned and prosperous, a personage like Oedipus, Thyestes, or other illustrious men of such families." The fate of such a man will excite not despair or shock, but pity and fear, pity "aroused by unmerited misfortune, fear by the misfortune of a man like ourselves."[5]

Sophocles was indeed the greatest of dramatists in this glorious age of tragedy. Adding a third actor, developing more fully the size and function of the chorus, working on a more ample concept of scenery and costuming, intensifying the poetic quality of drama, he made theater a more exciting experience. Yet it is his tragic sense that captures us most and conveys to us—especially in the context of these lectures—the texture and feeling of Greek tragedy. Although he is the author of many plays, we are most drawn to *Antigone* and *Oedipus the King*, and they will be our major concern.

Born in 495 B.C. and living until 406 B.C., Sophocles, like Euripides, knew the full blush of Athens' greatness, but also lived to see its decline—the development of a wealthy ruling oligarchy, the Sophists' attack on belief, the imperialistic ambitions, the ultimate weakening of the city-state—both financially and militarily—during the long Peloponnesian War (431-404 B.C.). In a word, he knew greatness and decline, the tradition and the challenge. The mood of his plays is notably different. It is as if he strikes middle ground between the conservatism of Aeschylus and the radicalism of Euripides. His is a more humanistic tragedy, one more concerned with human problems—Antigone's struggle between law and conscience, Oedipus' need to know his identity. It is a richer tragedy with more emphasis on character, drama, art generally. Is it any wonder that Sophocles is cited so often in Aristotle's *Poetics* as an exemplar of some peculiar excellence in the tragic form?

We focus on just two of Sophocles' plays to capture briefly the Sophoclean vision of tragedy. Both offer us creatures of magnitude—Oedipus, King of Thebes, and his daughter Antigone. Both possess not simply aristocratic bearing, but a certain largeness of spirit. Both are basically noble, good, and yet both have a kind of humanity about them that is capable of impetuosity, of lack of judgment, of rash action, of wanting to take on more than human powers. Both have Aristotle's tragic flaw, a flaw which ultimately brings disaster. Yet their downfall is not without meaning, without a sense of awareness. We as audience witness their downfall; we pity and we fear, and yet— most important—we sense the grandeur with which they meet their fate and come to terms with human limitation, with the mystery of divine power.

Sophocles turned to the great Oedipus myth for his Theban plays, giving that myth his own special interpretation and presentation. Most of us know the general outlines of that myth. An oracle warns King Laius of Thebes about the birth of a son who will slay him. In his fear he orders the killing of the child, but a shepherd, instead of carrying out the order, abandons him, and he is rescued by a shepherd of Corinth, brought to Corinth, and adopted by King Polybus and Queen Merope. Learning of the curse under which he lives, Oedipus leaves Corinth, coming again to Thebes after unwittingly killing his true father Laius in a fight at a crossroads. Solving the riddle of the Sphinx, he arrives in Thebes, becomes King, again unwittingly marries the dead King's wife and his own mother, Jocasta, and fathers two daughters—sisters Antigone and Ismene—and two sons— brothers Eteocles and Polyneices.

Calamity has come to Thebes in the form of plague, and it is at this point that the play begins. The citizens look to their new King Oedipus to cleanse the land, and hence emerges a master- piece of ironic plotting, the man in search of himself. Oedipus is truly the man of magnitude, obviously kingly, but also brave, caring, yet terribly human in his impetuosity. We listen first to the Priest of Zeus, speaking for the people:

> Nay, Oedipus, ruler of my land, thou seest of what years we are who beset thy altars,—some, nestlings still too tender for far flights, some, bowed with age, priests, as I of Zeus,—and these, the chosen youth . . .
> For the city, as thou thyself seest, is now too sorely vexed, and can no more lift her head from beneath the angry waves of death; a blight is on her in the fruitful blossoms of the land, in the herds among the pastures, in the barren pangs of women . . .
> And now, Oedipus, king glorious in all eyes, we beseech thee, all we suppliants, to find for us some succour, whether by the whisper of a god thou knowest it, or haply as in the power of man.

And we hear the graciousness and magnanimity of Oedipus's response:

> Oh my piteous children, known, well known to me are the desires wherewith ye have come: well wot I that ye suffer all; yet, sufferers as ye are, there is not one of you whose suffering is as mine. Your pain comes on each one of you for himself alone, and for no other; but my soul mourns at once for the city, and for myself, and for thee.

Oedipus slowly but relentlessly pursues the root of the plague, quizzing Creon who has returned from the oracle at Delphi with the word that the defilement of the land can be removed only by finding the killer of Laius. Harassing the soothsayer Teiresias until he reveals, "I say that thou art the slayer of the man whose slayer thou seekest," ignoring the warnings of Jocasta not to pursue the case further, he is drawn toward the staggering recognition—confirmed by the ancient shepherds of Corinth and Thebes—that the baby they exchanged was indeed Oedipus, that he had in fact killed his father Laius and married his mother Jocasta.

In a scene of great dramatic intensity reported by a messenger, Oedipus—Jocasta having killed herself in terror—blinds himself with the brooches of her garment. The final sight of the blinded King is almost overwhelming; here is the true tragic hero, man, who would aspire to godlike knowledge, now fully human, pleading for the well-being of his daughters, calm after passionate searching, ironically seeing the truth in the midst of his blindness. To the Chorus, he speaks words of self-knowledge not heard earlier:

> Show me not at large that these things are not best done thus: give me counsel no more. For, had I sight, I know not with what eyes I could e'en have looked on my father, when I came to the place of the dead, aye, or on my miserable mother, since against both I have sinned such sins as strangling could not punish. But deem ye that the sight of children, born as mine were born, was lovely for me to look upon? No, no, not lovely to mine eyes for ever! No, nor was this town with its towered walls, nor the sacred statues of the gods, since I, thrice wretched that I am,—I, noblest of the sons of Thebes,—have doomed myself to know these no more, by mine own command that all should thrust away the impious one—even him whom gods have shown to be unholy—and of the race of Laius!

With Creon we say, "Thy grief hath had large scope enough" and "Crave not to be master in all things: for the mastery which thou didst win hath not followed thee through life." There is a calm that tempers the horror of Oedipus' predicament, a calm more fully seen and felt in *Oedipus at Colonus,* the last of the Theban plays, where twenty years later with Creon now king, Oedipus becomes a charmed figure passing through the land to a blessed end. The final choral ode seems to enforce the calm, to temper the tragic fear evoked by the final spectacle of Oedipus. It is an ode which sings of the great man who meets suffering and of the association of that man with all of us:

> Dwellers in our native Thebes, behold this is Oedipus, who knew the famed riddle, and was a man most mighty; on whose fortunes what citizen did not gaze with envy? Behold into what a stormy sea of dread trouble he hath come!
> Therefore, while our eyes wait to see the destined final day, we must call no man happy who is of mortal race, until he hath crossed life's border, free from pain.

Antigone, a play which has become a standard for high school students and for college undergraduates, largely because of the vitality of its central tension between the state and the individual, law and conscience, picks up the Oedipus myth at a much later date. Eteocles, son of Oedipus and now King of Thebes, has ousted his brother Polyneices in a power struggle. Polyneices in exile launches a mighty army against Thebes, and in the battle both brothers are killed, fulfilling the prophecy of their father Oedipus. Creon now assumes the throne, a man of magnitude but almost excessively virtuous, suspicious, tied to the law, unwilling to listen and to see the human side of a situation. The action of the play takes place on the day after the battle as Creon declares that Eteocles be buried with all the rites of honor and Polyneices be left to rot on the battleground without burial.

The roots of this plot in ancient ideas of ritual burial are, of course, clear, but what gives the play its largeness of scope, its universal significance is the struggle that ensues between Creon —king, protector of the land, enforcer of the law—and Antigone —noble woman, loving sister devoted to the "right." It is this passionate struggle, this awful gulf between human beings unable to communicate and in the process meeting disaster that draws us to *Antigone.* Superb characterization; the delicate artistry that involves the chorus in the action; language, imagery, music—all of these enhance the great struggle.

And yet there are no easy answers in the play. Creon is, on the one hand, the bloodless ruler, the enforcer of law in the abstract. We listen to his words to the Leader of the Chorus and see this side of his nature:

> No man can be fully known, in soul and spirit and mind, until he hath been versed in rule and law-giving . . .
>
> . . . .
>
> Such are the rules by which I guard this city's greatness. And in accord with them is the edict which I have now published to the folk touching the sons of Oedipus;—that Eteocles, who hath fallen fighting for our city, in all renown of arms, shall be entombed, and crowned with every rite that follows the noblest dead to their rest. But for his brother, Polyneices,—who came back from exile,

30

and sought to consume utterly with fire the city of his fathers and the shrines of his fathers' gods . . . it hath been proclaimed to our people that none shall grace him with sepulture or lament, but leave him unburied, a corpse for birds and dogs to eat, a ghastly sight of shame.

Creon will listen to no one, not even his beloved son Haimon, to no argument, even to Antigone's most forceful cry of love for a dead brother whose unburied body will forever be a source of shame to her. And yet there is that dimension of humanity in him which finally yields to the pleading of Teiresias and the reasoning of the Chorus, but only when it is too late to save Antigone and his wife and son. His final words are powerful indictments of himself and his fate:

Woe for the sins of a darkened soul, stubborn sins, fraught with death! Ah, ye behold us, the sire who hath slain, the son who hath perished! Woe is me, for the wretched blindness of my counsels! Alas, my son, thou hast died in thy youth, by a timeless doom, woe is me! —thy spirit hath fled,—not by thy folly, but by mine own!

. . . .

Ah me, I have learned the bitter lesson! But then, methinks, oh then, some god smote me from above with crushing weight, and hurled me into the ways of cruelty, woe is me,—overthrowing and trampling on my joy! Woe, woe, for the troublous toils of men!

Antigone is, on the one hand, a spectacular tragic heroine, bright, articulate, unafraid, willing to sacrifice everything— even her life—for her conscience. Her response to Creon is ringing as he asks if she has broken the law:

Yes; for it was not Zeus that had published me that edict; not such are the laws set among men by the Justice who dwells with the gods below; nor deemed I that thy decrees were of such force, that a mortal could override the unwritten and unfailing statutes of heaven. For their life is not of to-day or yesterday, but from all time, and no man knows when they were first put forth.

. . . .

31

So for me to meet this doom is trifling grief; but if I had suffered my mother's son to lie in death an unburied corpse, that would have grieved me; and for this, I am not grieved. And if my present deeds are foolish in thy sight, it may be that a foolish judge arraigns my folly.

And yet so often Antigone seems her father's daughter—stubborn, unyielding, cruel in her response to her sister Ismene's counsels for prudence and moderation. She seems almost too much the self-conscious martyr as she rejects Ismene's decision to die with her: "Share not thou my death, nor claim deeds to which thou hast not put thy hand; my death will suffice."

In a sense we see two kinds of tragic heroism. Creon seems closer to the Aristotelian ideal of the great man trapped by a flaw and unable to see the rashness of its nature until it is too

The theater of Epidaurus, Greece, regarded by many scholars as the most nearly perfect of the Greek theaters, was also the site for many performances of the tragedies.

late and his loved ones have perished. Antigone, like her father Oedipus, seems more sharply caught in the ancient family curse as she carries out with unbending devotion the burial of her brother. Unlike Creon who comes to terms with his pride and wrath, Antigone meets death single-mindedly, convinced that there can be no compromise with conscience, that there are evils greater than death.

In *Oedipus the King* and *Antigone* we see Sophoclean—one might say Greek—tragedy at its height, underlining man's position in the scheme of things, a human being to be sure but with godlike possibilities. We see Sophocles' essential humanism, his idea of piety, of seeing the limits of reason and of tempering reason with feeling. As Cedric Whitman puts it, "Euripides asserts that the gods must behave in accord with man's morality in order to retain the divine title, but on the other hand he treats man as a weak and passion-driven creature: is it by this standard that he would measure all things? Sophocles asserts merely the divinity of the heroic soul. The hero had always been near to the gods; in Sophocles he is nearer than before. Only so can man really be the measure of all things, if the divine idea is in himself. The little man, who is the man of Euripides, can measure nothing. The great man is the real standard of the fifth century."[6]

We leave these dramas not without hope although the suffering at times appears unbearable, but with the vision of great human beings who suffer unjustly but whose suffering ennobles and instructs. We leave often with the stunning poetry of one of the great choral odes of *Antigone* ringing in our ears:

Wonders are many, and none is more wonderful than man; the power that crosses the white sea, driven by the stormy south-wind, making a path under surges that threaten to engulf him; and Earth, the eldest of the gods, the immortal, the unwearied doth he wear, turning the soil with the offspring of horses, as the ploughs go to and fro from year to year.

And as we reflect on the drama of Sophocles, on Greek tragedy at its best, we are left with the sense of the mystery of things, the enigmatic plight of human beings who suffer and yet endure. We are enriched by this spectacle, and we see our situation as lesser mortals more clearly. Tragedy's beginnings in fifth-century B.C. Athens are indeed auspicious.

NOTES

1. *Paideia: The Ideals of Greek Culture,* 3 vols., tr. from the second German edition by Gilbert Highet (New York: Oxford University Press, 1945), p. 4.

2. *The Greek Way* (New York: New American Library, 1948), p. 40.

3. *Greek Tragedy: A Literary Study* (Garden City, New York: Doubleday and Co., 1954), p. 307.

4. All quotations from the Greek tragedies are from *The Complete Greek Drama,* ed. Whitney J. Oates and Eugene O'Neill, Jr., 2 vols. (New York: Random House, 1938).

5. The translation of the *Poetics* is by S. H. Butcher and is found in *Criticism: The Major Texts,* ed. Walter Jackson Bate (New York: Harcourt Brace Jovanovich, 1970), pp. 19-39.

6. *Sophocles: A Study in Heroic Humanism* (Cambridge, Mass.: Harvard University Press, 1951), p. 99.

CHAPTER 2

Shakespeare and English Renaissance Tragedy

> "Caitiff, to pieces shake,
> That under covert and convenient seeming
> Has practiced on man's life. Close pent-up
> guilts,
> Rive your concealing continents and cry
> These dreadful summoners grace, I am a man
> More sinned against than sinning."
>
> *King Lear*

MUCH has been made early and late about the "great era" theory in the history of tragedy, and we will have more occasion to discuss it as we deal with nineteenth and twentieth-century drama. The tragedy of fifth-century B.C. Athens stands, of course, as the beginning, and for some the perfection of drama. Following great periods of tragedy, so the argument goes, there are fallow periods when the spectacle of great heroes and heroines struggling grandly with their fates before awe-struck audiences seems strangely absent.

There is, without being unduly deterministic or cyclic in our approach, something persuasive and attractive about this theory, certainly in the period following the decline and fall of Athens. Clearly a long period of decline followed the work of Euripides, the last of the great Greek tragedians. There seems little terribly fresh or original about the tragic drama of Rome. Is it the familiar ring of an eclectic Roman culture, more conservative, less venturesome, less original? The name of Seneca is frequently cited, but so many of Seneca's plays seem more melodrama than tragedy, more rhetoric than poetry. But Rome is only the beginning of a larger period of decline, a period triggered to a great extent by ecclesiastical opposition to stage plays, the sense that such plays threatened the moral fabric of a culture.

Ironically the drama reemerged during the Middle Ages, growing out of ecclesiastical celebrations, especially the Solemn High Masses of great feast days like Easter, Christmas, Corpus Christi. Perhaps the most celebrated example is the *Quem Queritis* trope of the Easter liturgy, a short tableau-like dramatic piece reenacting the dialogue of the women and the angel at the tomb of Jesus on Easter Morning. Such tropes—usually performed on a platform just outside the altar rail—seemed to catch the theme of the Mass for the congregation, often so much so that the drama became more important than the religious celebration. Plays were gradually moved outside the Church, into the village square, then came under the patronage of the guilds. Two kinds of plays predominate, the mystery or miracle dealing with sacred history or the lives of saints; and—most popular—the morality play, a simple drama, usually allegorical, dramatizing, for example, the struggle of the body and soul, for the edification of audiences. Of these *Everyman* has become the most celebrated and is still performed.

Popularity unfortunately—or perhaps fortunately—meant growing secularization of plot, characterization—biblical in their origins—and the guilds, now the patrons, would set up platforms on wheels for performances, developing perhaps the first sense of road companies. Competition between various towns—York, Chester, Coventry, Wakefield—and cycles of plays were developed. The interlude—a short, realistic play of entertainment generally associated with John Heywood—is still another example of the secularization of the drama. With all of this comes still further growth of professional dramatists and actors.

Drama develops rapidly in the sixteenth century. With local laws making it necessary to perform outside of London, plays were generally performed in the courtyards of inns, and, interestingly enough the Elizabethan stage—Shakespeare's own Globe Theater included—evolved. The Globe was roughly round—we remember the often quoted "This wooden O" of *Henry V*—and, like all the theaters, open to the elements. A number of galleries were built around the inside wall of the building, and here those who could pay for better seats took their places. The open floor, the pit was occupied by the groundlings who were content to do without chairs or benches. The stage was a platform extending half-way into the open area, and spectators sat on three sides. It was a stage that provided great intimacy and immediacy and a more lively interaction of actors and audience than the picture-frame stage of so much modern drama.

Puritan opposition to the drama as an instrument of Satan made the plight of actors precarious for a time, and they banded together under the protection of royal patrons. Shakespeare, for example, belonged to the Lord Chamberlain's Men which later became the King's Men. Drama slowly blossomed with the coming of the great playwrights Thomas Kyd, Christopher Marlowe, and, of course, Shakespeare himself. Renaissance drama triumphs over many obstacles, and audiences begin to view an enormous variety of superior plays. It is to William Shakespeare and Shakespearean tragedy that we turn our attention in this lecture.

For a writer who stands as one of the greatest in English and, for that matter, world literature, Shakespeare remains somewhat of a mystery.[1] We know so much about his plays, so little about his life. Born in Stratford-upon-Avon, baptized on April 26, 1564, he was probably classically educated. He married Anne Hathaway on November 28, 1582, and fathered three children, Susanna, baptized on May 26, 1583, and twins, Hamnet and Judith, baptized on February 2, 1585. But then there is a great lack of information—and, romantic speculation about the period has run rife—until we hear of Shakespeare in London in 1592. Can we imagine young Shakespeare of Stratford—like his counterpart, the twentieth-century rural American playwright—leaving home to try his fortunes in New York, leaving his family to fulfill his dream, to work in the theater as an actor, a writer? Whatever we imagine, we have relatively little hard information. He probably came up to London in 1587 or 1588 and threw himself into the burgeoning theater world. He joined Lord Strange's company as an actor and playwright and seemed to have great success. He had early contact with theater-men like Edward Alleyn and Christopher Marlowe, perhaps the greatest playwright of the age, dead at 29 in a barroom brawl. In 1594 he became associated, as we have already mentioned, with the Lord Chamberlain's Men, a prominent theatrical company which in 1603 became the King's Men. Actor, writer, even part owner of the Globe Theater, he was above all a maker of plays, plays which extend from as early as 1588 until 1613. By 1612, although again records leave much room for speculation, he is back in Stratford, the country boy returned to his roots, dead in 1616, buried April 25, 1616, in the church at Stratford.

So much for the man, or maybe so little. But the play's the thing with Shakespeare, and his plays bespeak another great episode in our developing history of tragedy. It is not that he excelled only in tragedy, for his career moves from an early phase of apprenticeship of comedy and history, the late 1580's and early 1590's—*Love's Labour's Lost, The Comedy of Errors, Henry VI,* 3 parts; to a period of high romantic comedy, the great history plays, early tragedy—from 1595 to the turn of the century—*The Merchant of Venice, Much Ado About Nothing,* the two parts of *Henry IV, Romeo and Juliet;* to the period of the dark comedies—*Troilus and Cressida, Measure for Measure*—and the great tragedies—*Julius Caesar, Othello, Hamlet, King Lear, Macbeth, Antony and Cleopatra*—from the turn of the century to 1609; to the final and somewhat mysterious period of the tragi-comedies and romances—1610-1613—*Cymbeline, The Winter's Tale, The Tempest.*

It is in tragedy, Samuel Johnson notwithstanding, that Shakespeare achieved his greatest success, and it is tragedy that concerns us in this series of lectures on its persistence through the history of drama. Again we face the question of the time, the culture, not arguing for artistic determinism, but rather drawing attention to the flourishing of a second great period of tragedy in an era of political and intellectual achievement. The period is, of course, the English Renaissance of the sixteenth and early seventeenth century, that remarkable period of the revival of learning, the development of science, the flourishing of philosophy. A European phenomenon, to be sure, one that we associate with Europe and then with England, its effects in England were enormous. We are caught by the similarity between fifth-century Athens and England of the sixteenth century. The London that Shakespeare came to in the late 1580's was bursting at the seams, alive with industry, commerce, royal power, and—above all—the extension of knowledge brought back from the Continent. It was the Age of Elizabeth; she, as J. Dover Wilson has argued, was the great unifying principle. "The Renaissance," he contends, "was essentially an assertion of the spiritual emancipation of man from the religion, the social structure, the scholasticism of the Middle Ages."[2]

Overriding political and economic considerations are philosophical and religious ones. It is important to see Christian humanism as a vital aspect of the age, an age celebrating a certain order in the universe, an order rooted in the image of the great chain of being, in Ptolemy's vision of a geocentric, anthropocentric universe, an order in which humankind had a place, in which in George Herbert's lines, "More servants wait on man/Than he'll take notice of." Theodore Spenser in *Shakespeare and the Nature of Man,* a book that has stood the test of time and the advances of scholarship very well, explores this idea of order in great depth, in the universe, in man himself, in the body politic, arguing for interrelationships among the three.[3] The key image is that of man himself, no mere bundle of impulses, but a creature of dignity, free, capable of reason, with a body that reflects a soul or inner spirit. The body politic likewise possessed a principle of unity with the ruler seen as man of conscience and virtue committed to a society concerned with the well-being of all its members.

Spenser—citing Thomas Aquinas' *De Regimine Principium,* "therefore let the king recognize that such is the office which he undertakes, namely, that he is to be in the kingdom what the soul is to the body, and what God is in the world"—sees the three realms as interrelated, the cosmos explained by the body and the body explained by the state, and so on.

And yet to remain with only this image of the Renaissance of Shakespeare is to miss seriously the complexity of the age. The period of the great tragedies is late Renaissance, a period of transition and change in which the tradition persists but with new challenges. Medieval and Renaissance collide. The age of exploration and discovery brought America and other new lands into view. The explosion of knowledge continued apace, especially the widening and larger implications of scientific knowledge. The continuing post-Reformation struggle between

Anglican and Puritan, King and Parliament culminated in the destructive Puritan Revolution, Civil War, the killing of a king. The beginnings of modern astronomy, the new phenomena of spots on the sun, the moons of Jupiter; ideas of a plurality of worlds, of the decay of the world—these are but a few examples of that explosion. Galileo's telescope not only brought new worlds into view, but ultimately gave the lie to Ptolemy's cosmology and verified Copernicus' hypothesis about the solar system, that the earth is not the center but the sun, and that the earth, far from being the center of things, is just another remote planet whirling in space.

The image of man as creature of dignity gifted with the power of reason to know the truth is increasingly undermined. Michel de Montaigne's *Apology for Raymond Sebond,* often cited as the Bible of a new skepticism about man, emphasizes the flux of things, the vanity and puniness of man's attempts to know anything for certain by reason or sensation, the need for a kind of blind faith. The essentially pragmatic political philosophy of Machiavelli's *The Prince* challenged the earlier ideal of morality as chief measure of political rule and replaced it with power and the security of the state as guiding principles.

In this tradition-challenge conflict, familiar to us already from our consideration of fifth-century Athens, in this new challenge to the spiritual dimension of man, the order of things, the moral side of political rule, we see, however briefly sketched, something of the spirit of the age of Shakespeare's tragedies. "It was," says Spenser, "because Shakespeare, as he developed his art, was able to see individual experience in relation to the all-inclusive conflict produced by this violation, that his great tragedies have such wide reverberations and give us so profound a picture of the nature of man."[4]

We must, as always, resist the argument that the moment makes the work of art, that the kind of transition and challenge we have discussed necessarily produces a certain kind of tragedy. And yet, as in fifth-century Athens, so in Elizabethan England, we find a period of great philosophical, scientific and literary activity, a period of change in which older verities are being challenged by new speculations. To all of this we add the great surge of national consciousness—again reminiscent of fifth-century Athens—as England turns back the ominous threat of the Spanish Armada. Shakespeare, as Spenser and others have argued, was very much attuned to the time and, while always the artist, brought to the drama of the late period a sense of something in the culture that underlined human issues, conflict, the struggle of great men and women with themselves and the forces around them. We will study his art, but will be conscious of the age.

In an ideal setting we might explore the range of Shakespearean tragedy. In the context of these six lectures on tragedy —and even here we must summarize too much, quote too little, range too widely—we might focus on two, *Hamlet* and *King Lear*.

HAMLET

The time is turn-of-the-century. Shakespeare has achieved celebrity as a master of the history play and romantic comedy. And yet even here the dangers of arguing for a sudden beginning of tragedy are clear. As early as 1592 he had dramatized the downfall of Richard III, a Machiavellian villain too evil to evoke any genuine pity and fear as he moves relentlessly and murderously towards the throne. In *Richard II* the history element still keeps us in the framework of the War of the Roses although Shakespeare seems less interested in history, more interested in the fall of a weak, selfish, and pathetic king—in love with the idea of kingship but Lear-like, unwilling to accept its challenges; poetic in his Hamlet-like soliloquies, and yet almost always unable to translate his image into reality. Richard II, we say, is too weak to be tragic; perhaps a word like pathetic better describes him. *Julius Caesar* in 1599 is, in a sense, both history and tragedy, with Shakespeare apparently drawn, as in the earlier histories, to profound questions of character—the balance of good and evil, the fall of a man destined for greatness. If Richard III is simply too evil and Richard II too weak to be tragic in Aristotle's terms, then Brutus is too noble, too naively good and idealistic. It is again a tragedy of pathos as we watch—with sympathy—the excessively noble Brutus ensnared by the wily, envious, plotting Cassius into the conspiracy that culminates in the killing of Caesar.

Hamlet seems drenched in the tragic as we have been

attempting to get at the heart of that word and that spirit. The bitterness and cynicism of the so-called dark comedies—*Troilus and Cressida, All's Well That Ends Well, Measure for Measure* —is in the air. There is, of course, the element of history in *Hamlet,* but it now seems to be used as a backdrop as Shakespeare concentrates on the fascinating tragic character and theme, the mystery that has made the play one of the most intriguing ever written. Like the Greeks, Shakespeare did not invent his stories. The Hamlet legend takes us back to the twelfth century, to the *Historia Danica* of Saxo Grammaticus, to the 1576 original of the English story, the *Histoires Tragiques* of Belleforest, to a Hamlet play popular in England in Shakespeare's time, to the large tradition of revenge tragedy so popular in English Renaissance drama.

Sources, however, remain sources as Shakespeare—drawn to the central character—makes them his servants rather than masters. It is as if he sees the tragic potentialities in the young prince and makes them his own. Hamlet becomes for Shakespeare the Christian Renaissance nobleman, son, soldier, scholar only recently returned to court from the University of Wittenberg, a young man not simply well-educated, but thoughtful, contemplative, brooding, given to seeing and examining the many sides of a question. He is basically good, devoted to parents and friends, concerned about his kingdom, cherishing the life of the mind, aware of the Christian verities of eternal life, goodness, justice, love, duty. Still he is from the beginning —in a kind of Greekish way—marked by fate for trouble. We could argue—if we had world enough and time in these lectures —the long-debated case about his procrastination, but, as we shall see in our discussion of his actions, that can hardly be a tragic flaw in any specific sense. His is a world in which things happen to him until the magic moment when he decides "to take up arms against a sea of troubles."

Shakespeare creates the tragic mood quickly. The changing of the guard at midnight on the battlements at Elsinore brings an immediate sense of something wrong in the kingdom. The guards exchange remarks on a frightening phenomenon already seen twice as they kept the watch. They speak of the skepticism of Hamlet's friend Horatio, a scholar, about the appearance of ghosts until he finally confronts the apparition and becomes a believer, now with "the sensible and true avouch/Of mine own eyes." Not only a ghost, but as Marcellus quizzes him on whether the ghost resembles the recently departed King, Horatio replies:

> As thou art to thyself.
> Such was the very armor he had on,
> When he had the ambitious Norway combated:
> So frowned he once, when, in an angry parle,
> He smote the sledded Polacks on the ice:
> 'Tis strange.[5]

Another time, another place, another set of supernatural forces are recalled as he continues:

> A mote it is to trouble the mind's eye.
> In the most high and palmy state of Rome,
> A little ere the mightiest Julius fell,
> The graves stood tenantless, and the sheeted dead
> Did squeak and gibber in the Roman streets;
> As stars with trains of fire and dews of blood,
> Disasters in the sun; and the moist star,
> Upon whose influence Neptune's empire stands,
> Was sick almost to Doomsday with eclipse.
> And even the like precurse of feared events,
> As harbingers preceding still the fates
> And prologue to the omen coming on,
> Have heaven and earth together demonstrated
> Unto our climatures and countrymen.

One is reminded of Kenneth Burke's excellent analysis of Shakespeare's master plotting, particularly his building of suspense, as we leave the puzzled but persuaded Horatio and friends on the battlement resolved to seek out the recently returned Hamlet to tell him of their story.[6]

Things do not develop quickly. The scene shifts to the newly established King Claudius opening his new court with a somber Hamlet looking on, disillusioned by what he has observed. We quickly learn of the death of Hamlet's father, the succession of Claudius to the throne and his mother's rather hasty remarriage to Claudius, the sending of ambassadors to Norway to deal with the threat of young Fortinbras, the granting of kingly

Richard Burton as Hamlet in Shakespeare's play.

permission to Laertes—son of Polonius and brother of Hamlet's beloved Ophelia—to return to his studies in Paris, and Hamlet's decision to remain in Denmark. Hamlet remains, to be sure, but sadly, moved by the death of a father he idolized, distressed by a mother he idealized, an uncle he scorned, a kingdom eaten away by moral corruption. After Claudius' long formalities and Hamlet's grudging agreement to stay in Denmark, we see him alone, now the center of our attention, in melancholy black. We hear him in soliloquy—the tragic hero *in potentia*—a good man in a forbidding world, a poet translating his sense of immorality in images of physical corruption, his torment at the death of his father and the remarriage of his mother in high rhetorical flourish:

> O that this too too sullied flesh would melt,
> Thaw and resolve itself into a dew,
> Or that the Everlasting had not fixed
> His Canon 'gainst self-slaughter. Oh God, God,
> How weary, stale, flat, and unprofitable
> Seem to me all the uses of this world!
> Fie on't, ah fie, 'tis an unweeded garden
> That grows to seed. Things rank and gross in nature
> Possess it merely. That it should come to this:
> But two months dead, nay not so much, not two—
> So excellent a King, that was to this
> Hyperion to a satyr, so loving to my mother,
> That he might not beteem the winds of heaven
> Visit her face too roughly. Heaven and earth,
> Must I remember? Why, she would hang on him
> As if increase of appetite had grown
> By what it fed on; and yet, within a month—
> Let me not think on't! Frailty, thy name is woman—
> A little month, or ere those shoes were old
> With which she followed my poor father's body
> Like Niobe, all tears, why she, even she—
> O God! a beast that wants discourse of reason
> Would have mourned longer—married with
>   my uncle,
> My father's brother, but no more like my father
> Than I to Hercules. Within a month,
> Ere yet the salt of most unrighteous tears
> Had left the flushing in her galled eyes,
> She married. O, most wicked speed, to post

With such dexterity to incestuous sheets!
It is not, nor it cannot come to good,
But break my heart, for I must hold my tongue!

The court scene closes with this spectacle of the great man disillusioned with the state of the world, and is quickly followed by the arrival of Horatio and the others with the news of the appearance of his father's ghost. The intellectual, like Horatio, he must test reports, inquire, verify for himself. And so he—in a sense like his tragic predecessor Oedipus—must take on the burden of the people, must know the truth wherever that truth may lead, must perhaps find the root of the plague in Denmark. Without fear, "Why, what should be the fear?/I do not set my life at a pin's fee;/And for my soul, what can it do to that,/Being a thing immortal as itself?", he confronts the ghost, still uncertain as to whether it is good or bad—hearing "I am thy father's spirit," the promise to "a tale unfold whose lightest word/Would harrow up thy soul, freeze thy young blood," commanding, to the shock of Hamlet: "Revenge his foul and most unnatural murder," spelling out in detail Claudius' insidious course of action, the poisoning in all its detail, the seduction of Gertrude:

Thus was I, sleeping, by a brother's hand
Of life, of crown, of queen, at once dispatched,
Cut off even in the blossoms of my sin,
Unhouseled, disappointed, unaneled,
No reck'ning made, but sent to my account
With all my imperfections on my head.

The charge is clear; there is only one exception, but a vital one for a young son revolted by the spectacle of his much loved mother now the mistress of "a satyr," "no more like my father/Than I to Hercules."
He must swear to revenge,

But, howsomever thou pursuest this act,
Taint not thy mind, nor let thy soul contrive
Against thy mother aught. Leave her to heaven
And to those thorns that in her bosom lodge
To prick and sting her.

And he does swear—and pledges his friends to secrecy—but not without a sense of the awesome nature of his task, a sense of being in the wrong place at the wrong time: "O cursed spite,/ That ever I was born to set it right!" As the tragedy is set in motion, we say to ourselves, as we said in Greek tragedy: But where is the evil in an Oedipus, an Antigone, a Hamlet? Why do good men and women suffer? Is there justice in the world? With the Greeks, especially with Sophocles, there was the terrifying power of fate, the sense of being trapped by primal curses, of the sins of parents being visited on children. Increasingly there was the sense of a certain hybris, a certain overreaching that perhaps contributed to the downfall of the hero or heroine. With *Hamlet* there is certainly less emphasis on fate, a greater sense of freedom of choice, on the possibility of the Christian idea of sin. Still Hamlet doesn't seem fated nor does he seem to be a sinful man. H.D.F. Kitto argues that in both *Hamlet* and the Greek plays, "crime leads to crime, or disaster to disaster in this linear fashion, but in *Hamlet* it spreads in another way too, one which is not Greek: it spreads from soul to soul, as a contagion." For Kitto Hamlet lives in a different kind of tragic world from Aeschylus' Orestes, for example, "one which requires that we should see how the contagion gradually spread over his whole spirit and his conduct."[7] Is he an example of Aristotle's error in judgment? Are Hamlet's own earlier words on Denmark ironically illuminating?

> So oft it chances in particular men
> That, for some vicious mole of nature in them,
> As in their birth—wherein they are not guilty,
> (Since nature cannot choose his origin)
> By the o'ergrowth of some complexion,
> Oft breaking down the pales and forts of reason,
> Or by some habit that too much o'erleavens
> The form of plausive manners, that (these men
> Carrying, I say, the stamp of one defect,
> Being nature's livery, or fortune's star,)
> Their virtues else be they as pure as grace,
> As infinite as man may undergo—
> Shall in the general censure take corruption
> From that particular fault. The dram of evil
> Doth all the noble substance of a doubt,
> To his own scandal.

Whatever the answer to this most baffling of riddles, the young Hamlet's tragedy is set in motion, as he prepares his plan of action—to avenge his father's death. And yet there is still the sense of questioning, of anxiety about the ghost, of wanting to catch Claudius directly. That verification will be achieved through a feigning of madness, especially in his relations with Ophelia whom he loves, to secure secrecy, the plan to have the visiting players at court perform for Claudius an old play called "The Murder of Gonzago"—the events of the play paralleling the events surrounding the murder of his own father—and the ultimate horror of Claudius as he views the play. The play did indeed "catch the conscience of the King" as he now in his terror plans to remove Hamlet through the agency of two of Hamlet's old friends Rosencrantz and Guildenstern. Never the merely Machiavellian villain, Claudius sees his offense clearly, yet cannot give up the consequences of that offense. As Hamlet, summoned by his mother to her chamber, passes by a room in the castle, he comes upon Claudius and overhears his tormented act of contrition, "O, my offense is rank, it smells to heaven;/ It hath the primal eldest curse upon't/A brother's murder."

What an opportunity to do away with his uncle given his new resolve for revenge; the King is alone, unarmed, confessing his sins openly. Yet Hamlet, not the moral weakling, the pro-crastinator, and very much in the tradition of Renaissance revenge tragedy, pulls back, always the intellectual weighing the several consequences of an idea or action. "Now might I do it pat, now 'a his a-praying,/And now I'll do it," he says. Now is the time for revenge, for fulfilling his solemn obligation to his father. But there are two sides to the problem, Hamlet continues: "And so 'a goes to heaven,/And so am I revenged. That would be scann'd./A villain kills my father, and for that,/I, his sole son, do this same villain send/To heaven." Killing a sinner in the midst of repentance guarantees his salvation; a perfect revenge must kill both body and soul. There must be another way, he reasons. "Why, this is hire and salary, not revenge."

Off to his mother's bedroom he goes for the powerful con-frontation scene, the baring of his disappointment with this mother, his sense of loss of his father. Hardly the squeamish delayer, his first move after berating his mother is the action of a

48

tragic hero, drawing his sword and running it through Polonius—he believes it is Claudius—behind the arras. Frustrated by his failure in this action—"I took thee for thy better."—he then confronts his mother in one of the most forceful scenes of the play, one fraught with uncertainties, questions, ironies. Was Gertrude a party to her husband's death? Is her marriage to Claudius in any way understandable or justifiable? Is Hamlet's preoccupation with his mother normal? We listen to and watch the power of their responses and wonder. The young hero, caught in the prison of Denmark, charged with a solemn obligation to revenge, more and more isolated from his sources of hope and confidence, angrily challenges his mother's horror at the killing of Polonius with a seething "A bloody deed— almost as bad, good Mother,/As kill a king, and marry with his brother." The words "kill a king" stun Gertrude; she seems genuinely unaware of any murder, but Hamlet, almost out of control, pursues her dramatically with a picture of his father and a withering comparison of her past life with her present. Hamlet is a man possessed, Oedipus-like in his rage:

> Look here upon this picture, and on this,
> The counterfeit presentment of two brothers.
> See what a grace was seated on this brow:
> Hyperion's curls; the front of Jove himself . . .
>
> . . . .
>
> Look you now upon what follows,
> Here is your husband, like a mildewed ear
> Blasting his wholesome brother. Have you eyes?

It must be lust, charges Hamlet: "O shame, where is thy blush?"

Hamlet's verbal assault leaves Gertrude almost helpless; he would continue it until the Ghost appears in his mind's eye to temper his rage, to remind him of his earlier charge to leave her to the judgment of heaven. Persuaded of his madness, Gertrude listens to his words of counsel; she must, he says, gradually separate herself from the lustful advances of Claudius. "Once more, good night,/And when you are desirous I'll blessing beg of you."

The tragic sense of inevitability is now clear as the Queen reports her interview to Claudius. The resolve of Hamlet, the decision of Claudius to ship him to England with Rosencrantz and Guildenstern and to do away with him there, the death of Ophelia, the return of Laertes and the challenge to Hamlet—all these are a prelude to destruction. Claudius' nefarious plans for insuring Hamlet's death in the duel with a poison cup and poison sword backfire. Both Hamlet and Laertes perish from the sword; Gertrude unwittingly drinks the poison cup; Hamlet's last act is the killing of Claudius. A savage conclusion indeed; evil breeds evil; death brings death.

There is, however, as in Greek tragedy, as in Aristotle's words concerning purgation of pity and fear, a certain calm that transcends the awful wreckage of the play. The exchange of blessings with Laertes, the return of Fortinbras and the restoration of order to the kingdom, the touching command of the dying Hamlet to Horatio:

> If thou didst ever hold me in thy heart,
> Absent thee from felicity awhile,
> And in this harsh world draw thy breath in pain,
> To tell my story.

It is Shakespeare who accepts the charge to tell the story "Of carnal, bloody, and unnatural acts,/Of accidental judgements, casual slaughters,/Of deaths put on by cunning and forced cause,/And, in this upshot, purposes mistook/Fallen on th' inventors' heads." With Fortinbras, as Hamlet is borne to the stage, we say: "For he was likely, had he been put on,/To have proved most royal." Shakespeare's world has darkened at the turn of the century; *Hamlet* may be his first great tragedy. In this world of darkness young Hamlet, full of promise, destined for greatness, is ruined by the time, by the evil that surrounds him. The final effect seems to be one of enormous waste, yet there seems to be an even greater sense of the good and noble man who struggled to set the time right, to take up arms bravely against that sea of troubles. "The soldiers' music and the rites of war/Speak loudly for him."

With *King Lear* we move to 1604-1605, and again without resorting to any purely cyclic approach, we clearly note a new phase in Shakespeare's development as a tragedian. We have, as in *Hamlet*, moved beyond historical tragedy, beyond the play of fate. The tragedy now seems to move within the hero. In *Othello, King Lear, Macbeth, Antony and Cleopatra,* and *Coriolanus,* although fate plays its role, the tragic flaw in the individual plays an even greater one. And the tragic flaw increasingly involves more than an error in judgment; it seems a pronounced moral weakness, something approaching the Christian idea of sin—an inner and outer disorder. The disorder is individual, political, cosmic. The enemy within reflects the enemy without. L.C. Knights sees *King Lear* as "a universal allegory . . . , and its dramatic technique is determined by the need to present certain permanent aspects of the human situation, with a maximum of imaginative realization and a minimum regard for the conventions of naturalism."[8]

We focus on the play itself, and we have all the Aristotelian requirements for magnitude—kingship, personal stature, largeness of spirit, generosity. And yet the enemy within is clear from the beginning. The King—apparently a good one up to the time we meet him in the play—has grown older, has come to know the fear that comes with age. He has also become tyrannical, capable of great rage. Most of all he has become foolish, for Knights "the embodiment of perverse self-will."[9]

The opening of the play—like the opening of *Hamlet*—skillfully evokes a mood, a sense of things gone wrong. The seemingly incongruous opening exchange of Kent, Gloucester, and Edmund is hardly a conversation as we learn that the King has already decided on a division of the kingdom and strangely, according to Kent, "had more affected the Duke of Albany than Cornwall." But, says Gloucester, "it appears not which of the dukes he values most, for equalities are so weighed that curiosity in neither can make choice of either's moiety." It is a world of joking about lust as Kent, admiring the handsome Edmund, inquires of Gloucester: "Is not this your son, my lord?" to be answered with "His breeding, sir, hath been at my charge. I have so often blushed to acknowledge him, that now I am brazed to't." A puzzled Kent answers with "I cannot conceive you," to which a punning Gloucester retorts:

> Sir, this young fellow's mother could;
> Whereupon she grew round-wombed, and
> had indeed, sir, a son for her cradle ere
> she had a husband for her bed. Do you smell
> a fault?

Far from it, reacts Kent: "I cannot wish the fault undone, the issue of it being so proper."

In this context we witness the magnificent opening court scene as the aging King Lear, eager to free himself from the responsibilities but not the perquisites of leadership, decides on a competition among his daughters as a way of dividing the kingdom. It is a strange competition indeed—

> Tell me, my daughters
> (Since now we will divest us both of rule,
> Interests of territory, cares of state),
> Which of you shall we say doth love us most,
> That we our largest bounty may extend
> Where nature doth with merit challenge.

It is almost a perverse request rooted in pride or arrogance or perhaps in a growing inner insecurity. Two of the daughters, Goneril and Regan, are worldly-wise, however, aware of an erosion of their father's inner strength, and are ready with extravagant answers, with lavish protestations of their love for their father. And, as this world goes, their rewards are forthcoming; flattery will get them a third of the kingdom. Meanwhile as the competition proceeds, a third daughter, off to the side and distressed not only by the sycophancy of her sisters, but by her own inability to translate the depth of her daughterly love in rhetorical flourishes, broods, feels unable to respond as her father wants. Still, the other daughters' speeches sufficiently gratifying to a faltering ego, Lear turns to Cordelia, obviously his favorite daughter and interestingly enough the one for whom he has the choicest award: "what can you say, to draw/A third more opulent than your sisters? Speak."

52

But speak she cannot, at least cannot say what her father wants to hear. "Nothing, my lord," she replies, some would say a hard-hearted reply from a loving daughter to an aging father, others would say an honest one given her sense of honesty, given her unhappiness that "I cannot heave/My heart into my mouth." Lear, the great man, the King, is enraged, even at his favorite daughter, and focuses on that maddening word throughout the play—"Nothing." He simply cannot come to terms with this kind of terse language—"Nothing will come of nothing. Speak again." But further questioning, further appeals to her sense of the material advantages of a fulsome reply bring only Cordelia's:

> Good, my lord,
> You have begot me, bred me, loved me. I
> Return those duties back as are right fit,
> Obey you, love you, and most honour you.
> Why have my sisters husbands, if they say
> They love you all? Haply, when I shall wed,
> That lord whose hand must take my plight shall carry
> Half my love with him, half my care and duty.
> Sure I shall never marry like my sisters,
> To love my father all.

Lear moves from self-pity—"So young, and so untender?"—to rage—"Let it be so, thy truth then be thy dower/ . . . Here I disclaim all my paternal care,/Propinquity and property of blood,/And as a stranger to my heart and me/Hold thee from this forever." Even Kent, his loyal earl, cannot appeal to his sense of reason and justice, and, like Cordelia, is banished with a fierce "Out of my sight!" Little by little goodness leaves Lear's world, and the darkness of his isolation gathers. It is a world of great disorder, where everything is turned loose, truly a place "Where ignorant armies clash by night." As if to reinforce and parallel the Lear plot of ingratitude and injustice, the Gloucester story unfolds. Gloucester, a great if not as great a figure as Lear, is likewise hoodwinked by fast talk and clever cajolery. His bastard son Edmund, already alluded to in the opening scene, handsome, facilely verbal, ambitious in the extreme, resents the favor and legitimacy of his brother Edgar, and conspires to ruin him by insinuating that he is plotting against his father.

Paul Schofield as King Lear in Shakespeare's play.

Edmund's rhetoric, like Satan's in *Paradise Lost,* is wonderfully vital, dashingly conspiratorial. His is a mind turned away from love, an energy turned toward evil, a lust destructive in the extreme. His is a world topsy-turvy, a world without values, a world where all traditions are subject to challenge. It is a world in which Edgar, or Gloucester, or any good person, cannot survive for long. In soliloquy he prays to "Nature" as "my goddess," not nature as the Elizabethans might have viewed it, but as impulse, self-indulgence. He mocks the ruler of a society that deprives him, physically and intellectually attractive, of lawful sonship, of rights to title and property:

> Why brand they us
> With base? With baseness? Bastardy? Base? Base?
> Who, in the lusty stealth of nature, take
> More composition and fierce quality
> Than doth, within a dull, stale, tired bed,
> Go to th' creating a whole tribe of fops

Got 'tween sleep and wake? Well then,
Legitimate Edgar, I must have your land.

. . . .

Now, gods, stand up for bastards.

Edmund's resourcefulness is unbounded as he persuades his
father that his loyal son is in fact plotting against him, is
planning his murder in order to gain the family fortune. How
completely in control evil seems to be in Gloucester's world, as
in Lear's, as Edmund parodies his father's analysis of the discord
in the kingdom in terms of fate, of "These late eclipses in the
sun and moon." Ironically it is the villain who firmly believes in
free will, in the sinister initiation of evil by the free choice of the
individual.

> This is the excellent foppery of the world, that when we
> are sick in fortune, often the surfeit of our own behavior,
> we make guilty of our disasters the sun, the moon, and
> stars, as if we were villains on necessity; fools by heavenly
> compulsion; knaves, thieves, and treachers by spherical
> predominance; drunkards, liars, and adulterers by an
> enforced obedience of planetary influence; and all that we
> are evil in, by a divine thrusting on . . . Fut! I should have
> been that I am, had the maidenliest star in the firmament
> twinkled on my bastardizing.

With the introduction of the parallel plots, the tragedy is
intensified, and, even though Gloucester, Edmund, and Edgar
play their vital roles and draw us to them, it is Lear, like Hamlet,
who always seems center-stage, always seems the overwhelmingly large tragic hero. In his prideful rage he has banished
Cordelia, Kent—the forces of good, of honesty—and has been
taken in by the forces of appearance. Cordelia's love is
"nothing" for him; Goneril and Regan's flattery is everything.
The appearance has become the reality, and the reality is now
disorder, a great battle with the forces of evil unleashed and
seemingly unchecked. It is a world in which fathers are
deceived, sons and daughters disloyal, wives unfaithful. The
Fool catches it best as he mocks—albeit with love—his Master

hoodwinked, as he describes an Alice in Wonderland upside-down world.

The folly of his trust in appearance is quickly unfolded as his hopes for a carefree retirement—the trappings of kingship, the companionship of his drinking club, the disappearance of responsibility—are dashed. He will divide his leisure time between his daughters Regan and Goneril, or so he thinks. Goneril has felt he can do with a smaller retinue, and so he appeals to Regan, who would reduce it even further to twenty-five, then to ten to five to Regan's "What need one?" Regan's remark in the exchange is the cutting one: "I pray you, father, being weak, seem so."

Lear's outburst is classic:

> O reason not the need! Our basest beggars
> Are in the poorest thing superfluous
> Allow not nature more than nature needs,
> Man's life is cheap as beast's.

Near madness, cast out into the raging storm by his daughters, vowing revenge on them, Lear, the great man who had believed himself to be godlike, above love, family, everything, is now a ravaged spirit. And again his situation is brilliantly reinforced by Gloucester's who, having banished his good son Edgar now disguised as the mad Tom O'Bedlam, his guide, finds himself betrayed by the appearance of Edmund, blinded, and banished. Lear, reduced to a mere survival-existence, surrounded by figures of goodness like Kent and Edgar, achieves a kind of vision in madness, commanding the elements with a wild exuberance, pulling off his clothes, listening to the crazy good sense of the Fool. There are few more powerful speeches than Lear's response to the dishevelled appearance and ranting gibberish of the mad Tom:

> Thou wert better in a grave than to answer with thy uncovered body this extremity of the skies. Is man no more than this? Consider him well. Thou ow'st the worm no silk, the beast no hide, the sheep no wool, the cat no perfume. Ha? Here's three on's are sophisticated. Thou art the thing itself; unaccommodated man is no more but such a poor, bare, forked animal as thou art. Off, off, you lendings! Come, unbutton here.

Skillfully plotted, the play moves to its physical and spiritual center on the heath. Naked, alone, deprived, the two towering figures of Gloucester and Lear encounter one another, one physically blind, the other spiritually, both stripped of everything and reduced to borderline status as human beings. Can they suffer any more? Is the world totally out of control? Will they both go mad and send us out of the theater with a sense that their world is absurd, that death will follow madness, that everything ultimately is a sort of cruel, cosmic blackness, "the horror."

It is an astonishing meeting, tragic to be sure, but tragic in that Aristotelian—now Shakespearean—sense that leaves us not with hopelessness but with a sense of slow purgation. There is no poetic justice, but a higher justice as Lear and Gloucester come to terms with themselves, discover their own blindness, learn that the appearance was wrong, that the realities of Cordelia and Edgar were right. It is a wild scene worthy of Beckett as Lear, bedecked with weeds and flowers, meets the blinded, bloodied Gloucester, Lear beside himself as he plays a number of imaginary roles, Gloucester responding with amazement and awe. Lear's rhetoric seems to challenge all values. The man taken in adultery shall not die. "Die for adultery? No:/The wren goes to't, and the small gilded fly/Does lecher in my sight./ Let copulation thrive."

Lear is slowly cleansed of his anger, his near-nihilism. A slow process of regeneration begins as he—once proud, vain, godlike in his pretensions—must be recognized before some kind of order can be restored. Lear wildly decries his daughters, and yet interestingly recognizes himself:

Ha! Goneril with a white beard! They flattered me like a dog, and told me I had white hairs in my beard, ere the black ones where there. To say "ay," and "no," to everything that I said. "Ay," and "no" too was no good divinity. When the rain came to wet me once, and the wind to make me chatter; when the thunder would not peace at my bidding; there I found 'em, there I smelt 'em out. Go to, they are not men o' their words: they told me I was everything. 'Tis a lie, I am not ague-proof.

Gloucester, touched by the voice of Lear, would kiss the King's hand, only to have Lear pull back with "Let me wipe it first, it smells of mortality." Lear learns finiteness; the beginnings of redemption are there. There will, of course, be no sentimental victory even though Cordelia and France return to restore some kind of order to a diseased kingdom. And diseased it is with Goneril and Regan vying for supremacy and the lustful love of Edmund. It is—with Albany the only exception—a kingdom of wantonness, self-seeking. In the midst of it all is the reunion of Cordelia and Lear, daughter and father, in a scene so heart-breaking as to be almost unbearable. And yet what dominates in the end is love, love the root of Cordelia's forgiveness, "O look upon me, sir,/And hold your hand in benediction o'er me./You must not kneel," and Lear's recognition, "Pray, do not mock me: I am a very foolish fond old man." Taken prisoners by the forces of Goneril, Regan, and Edmund, Lear pleads with Cordelia for a kingdom of their own, a paradise of love in a world where love has been avoided: "No, no, no, no! Come, let's away to prison:/We two alone will sing like birds i' the' cage:/When thou dost ask me blessing, I'll kneel down/And ask of thee forgiveness."

Lear and Cordelia die as they must in the scheme of things, but the forces of good prevail. Edmund is defeated by Edgar, Goneril and Regan by their own lust. The strange vision at the end of the play—Albany, Edgar, Kent, the forces of good returning after exile—seems like an embodiment of Shake-spearean tragedy. A great storm has disrupted the elements, but has blown itself out and in the process purified things. Men and women have violated, suffered, but have also learned something of the mystery of the human situation. A central heroic figure has been caught by a tragic flaw and has perished, but there has been a nobility and growth in the perishing. Edgar's earlier exchange with his father seems to catch so much of the spirit of tragedy. Edgar says, "Away, old man; give thy hand; away!/King Lear hath lost, he and his daughter ta'en:/Give me thy hand. Come on." Gloucester cannot accept this situation, saying "No further, sir; a man may rot even here," only to hear Edgar's eloquent concern and consolation: "What, in ill thoughts again? Men must endure/Their going hence, even as their coming hither,/Ripeness is all." Stephen Booth in a recent essay on *King Lear* offers a brilliant analysis of the play's ending. "The way of our escape and Lear's are one. We *want* Lear to die, just as almost from the beginning, we have wanted the play to end. That does not mean that we are unfeeling toward Lear or that we dislike the play: watching *Lear* is not unlike waiting for the death of a dying friend; our eagerness for the end makes the friend no less dear."[10] Commenting on how the play turns out "to be faithless to the chronicle accounts of Lear," how revisions of the play to include happy endings—especially the eighteenth-century version of Nahum Tate—are unsatisfactory, Booth argues:

> To allow Lear and Cordelia to retire with victory and felicity would be to allow *more* to occur, would be to allow the range of our consideration and of our standards of evaluation to dilate infinitely. It would be a strong man whose natural ideas of justice and hopes for a happy resolution could outweigh his more basic need—his simple need for an ending—if, instead of Tate, he had seen Shakespeare.[11]

In *King Lear* we see the perfection of Shakespearean tragedy, perhaps the perfection of tragedy itself. The Greek backgrounds are there, the great man buffeted by the slings and arrows of an outrageous world, the man of magnitude caught by circumstance, more sinned against than sinning, the man condemned to suffer and yet meeting that suffering grandly and in the process coming to some new level of understanding. Shakespeare—as was so often the case with the Greeks—raised to a new level the power of tragedy to purge the emotions of pity and fear, not to leave the audience without hope. L.C. Knights, wrestling with the religious dimension of the play, with the play as exemplifying Shakespeare's Renaissance Christian humanism, offers a stunning description of the final vision of the play. Yes, Lear has reached a new sense of himself, but he has not been offered some kind of external support to which he clings. He has come to the boundary line, to the dark place, and sees himself anew. "The positives," says Knights, "that emerge from the play are indeed fundamental Christian values, but they are reached by an act of profound individual exploration: the play does not take them for granted; it takes nothing for granted but Nature and natural energies and passions." We are reminded of

Keats's remarkable observation: "the excellence of every Art is its intensity, capable of making all disagreeables evaporate from their being in close relationship with Beauty and Truth— Examine King Lear & you will find this exemplified throughout."

We leave the Shakespearean tragedy not with a sense of solution, of justice prevailing, but often with the feeling that we have watched one of our own struggling against formidable enemies, internal and external, frequently failing, often meeting death. And yet we do not despair because the hero has shown us both the limits and the possibilities of mortality, and we are richer human beings for having been spectators and participants in the process.

NOTES

1. An invaluable guide to biographical materials is S. Schoenbaum, *Shakespeare's Lives* (New York: Oxford University Press, 1970).

2. *The Essential Shakespeare: A Biographical Adventure* (Cambridge at the University Press, 1964), p. 18.

3. (New York: The Macmillan Company, 1958). I am greatly indebted to Spenser's telling analysis of the intellectual and scientific conflicts of Shakespeare's age.

4. Spenser, p. 50.

5. All quotations from the plays are from *The Complete Signet Classic Shakespeare,* General Editor Sylvan Barnet (New York: Harcourt Brace Jovanovich, Inc., 1972).

6. See "Psychology and Form" in Burke's *Counter-Statement* (Los Altos, California: Hermes Publications, 1931), pp. 29-44.

7. "Hamlet" in *Shakespeare Criticism, 1935-1960.* Selected with an Introduction by Anne Ridler (New York: Oxford University Press, 1970), pp. 164-165.

8. "King Lear" in Ridler, p. 263.

9. Ridler, p. 264.

10. Stephen Booth, *King Lear, Macbeth, Indefinition, and Tragedy* (New Haven and London: Yale University Press, 1983).

11. Booth, p. 57.

CHAPTER 3

Ibsen and the Beginnings of Modern Tragedy

> "Yes, yes—don't let us talk any more about the old days. You are buried up to your eyes now in committees and all sorts of business; and I am here, fighting with ghosts both without and within me."
>
> *Ghosts*

O UR topic is again a formidable one, perhaps much too large to be taken up in one lecture or even a series of lectures. If we make no claim to comprehensiveness, however, but try only to focus on another episode in the history of drama, perhaps we can suggest in useful ways the decline of tragedy after Shakespeare and its new beginnings in nineteenth-century Europe in the work of Henrik Ibsen.

We certainly do not exaggerate when we speak of decline even in Shakespeare's own time, to say nothing of the two-hundred years or so after his death. The Jacobean period offers us a tragedy of unrelieved evil and melodrama—of John Webster's *The Duchess of Malfi,* of Thomas Middleton's *The Changeling,* of John Ford's *'Tis a Pity She's a Whore*—and of great tragi-comedy, especially in the plays of Beaumont and Fletcher. The Puritan predominance, with its hostility to theatrical performances already noted, becomes firmly established and culminates in the closing of the theaters altogether for a time. There is little sign of the tragic paradigm as we have been considering it, or indeed of an artistic vision.

With the end of the Puritan Revolution and the Restoration of King Charles II, there follows a period of Enlightenment optimism, of a belief in progress, in the capacity of reason to deal with every question, even the ultimate questions of suffering and mystery. Pope's wonderful lines from *An Essay on Man,* while not necessarily a manifesto for a complex age, nevertheless capture some of the spirit of the age:

> Cease, then, nor order imperfection name:
> Our proper bliss depends on what we blame.
> Know thy own point: this kind, this due degree
> Of blindness, weakness, Heaven bestows on thee.
> Submit, in this, or any other sphere,
> Secure to be as blest as thou canst bear:
> Safe in the hand of one Disposing Power,
> Or in the natal, or the mortal hour.
> All Nature is but art, unknown to thee
> All chance, direction, which thou canst not see;
> All discord, harmony not understood;
> All partial evil, universal good:
> And, spite of pride, in erring reason's spite,
> One truth is clear. Whatever is, is right.

Given these premises, there seemed little room for the searching questions that preoccupied the Greeks and Shakespeare as, caught between two traditions, two images of man, they sought to raise and deal with these questions. Is there a supreme power, an order in the nature of things? Does man have a meaning? Why is there suffering in a world supposedly under the protection of divine agency? Instead we have in England the sentimental drama of Henry Fielding and Oliver Goldsmith, the satires of Richard Sheridan, the smugness of Restoration Comedy, with its assuaging of courtly manners and morals, the heroic drama of Dryden and Otway. In France there is, of course, the neoclassic heroic tragedy of Racine with its "destructive passion" and of Corneille with its "great deed," but such drama seemed too formal, too removed from the central human questions of tragedy as we have been studying it.

The Romantics reversed the process, but came no closer to a tragic center. The new hero is the man of feeling trapped in an unsympathetic world. Goethe's Werther and Faust, Byron's Childe Harold and Manfred, Shelley's Prometheus—these are stunning examples of the new hero, pained, egotistical in the extreme, seeking liberation through isolation from the world, travel, the solace of lonely places. Tragedy becomes a vehicle for the self-expression of the hero, for the delicate analysis of the ennui, boredom and frustration of spirit. There is little sense of the world beyond, of growth, of suffering as a vehicle for fuller awareness of the human situation. Byron's Manfred captures much of the mood:

> We are the fools of time and terror: Days
> Steal on us and steal from us; yet we live,
> Loathing our life, and dreading still to die.
> In all the days of this detested yoke—
> This vital weight upon the struggling heart,
> Which sinks with sorrow, or beats quick with pain,
> Or joy that ends in agony or faintness—
> In all the days of past and future, for
> In life there is no present.

We wonder whether "pathetic" rather than "tragic" is the more appropriate word for such drama.

It was this drama of the individual, this tragedy of the Rousseauistic naturally good man ruined by the evil that surrounded him that held the center of the stage for the first part of the nineteenth century. The poetry is often magnificent, the soliloquies eloquent, but there is little dramatic conflict as the expanding consciousness of the central character dominates, indeed overwhelms us. That image of the towering individual —an image inspired largely by the French Revolution and the anti-Industrial Revolution return to nature—the hero challenging the elements, summoning spirits was to be somewhat eroded by the events of the future, the collapse of the Revolution, the Reign of Terror, the reactionary post-Revolution settlements. A new sadness, a new disillusionment sets in, epitomized especially in the memorable last stanza of Matthew Arnold's "Dover Beach":

> Ah, love, let us be true
> To one another! for the world, which seems
> To lie before us like a land of dreams,
> So various, so beautiful, so new,
> Hath really neither joy, nor love, nor light,
> Nor certitude, nor peace, nor help for pain;
> And we are here as on a darkling plain

Swept with confused alarms of struggle and flight,
Where ignorant armies clash by night.

Joseph Wood Krutch, the distinguished literary critic, has argued that there was a "grand strategy at work in later nineteenth and earlier twentieth century thought, one that had as its aim "the destruction of man's former belief in his own autonomy." The villains in the piece are Darwinian biology, Marxian economics, and Freudian psychology. "Each emphasized the extent to which the human being is the product of forces outside his control." All of these were, of course, great pioneering forces, but accepting their hypotheses "meant to emphasize strongly if not exclusively the extent to which he has played a passive role and to encourage him to see himself as essentially not merely a 'product' but also a victim."[1]

Solidly in the midst of this nineteenth-century post-Romantic reaction is Henrik Ibsen, the subject of this lecture who, along with August Strindberg and George Bernard Shaw, dominated the drama of the period.

Born in Skien, Norway on March 20, 1828 about a hundred miles from Christiania (now Oslo), Ibsen came from a family which lost its wealth and social status shortly after his birth. The family moved to a farm where Ibsen had an unhappy adolescence, especially since he could find no outlet for his creative talents. He left home as a sixteen-year-old, became an apothecary's apprentice in a village at Grimstad. Caught up in all the revolutionary causes sweeping across Europe in the middle of the century, he abandoned the idea of a career in medicine and started to write, a vocation that brought little early success. He served for a time as dramatist, director for the Norwegian Theater at Christiania which failed in 1862. These were years of struggle, failure, poverty after which Ibsen moved to Rome where the great plays we associate with him were written. A celebrity in spite of the controversial nature of the plays of these twenty-five years, he returned to Norway in 1891, died in Christiania on May 23, 1906.

It is in the plays of the so-called later period that we find Ibsen crucial for our discussion of tragedy. Some would indeed call him the father of modern tragedy with all the implications of the word modern. Clearly the world of *A Doll's House* (1879), *Ghosts* (1881), *An Enemy of the People* (1882), *The Wild Duck* (1884), *Hedda Gabler* (1890) is a very different one from those of Shakespeare and Sophocles. Nora Helmer and her bank-manager husband Torvald, Mrs. Alving and Pastor Manders, Dr. Stockman, the doomed Ekdal family, the romantic, languorous Hedda and her pedant husband George Tessman—these and so many others seem ordinary compared to Oedipus the King, Antigone, Hamlet, King Lear. The settings—generally living rooms, studies—are more realistic. Gone are the poetry, the choral odes, and rhetoric of the Greeks and Shakespeare; we hear the language of real men and women, especially in the good translations. Gone are the struggles of gods and humans, the encounters of royal princes with fate as we witness a more social drama with problems that touch a modern audience in more immediate ways—Nora breaking out of her loveless marriage to a man interested only in respectability, Dr. Stockman fighting for a clean environment, Mrs. Alving protecting the respectability of a family, Hedda Gabler seeking some creative outlet in the midst of a marriage of convenience to the dull, unimaginative scholar George Tessman.

Ibsen is indeed modern in that he has brought tragedy closer in some ways to his audience. Some claim too close, so close that the subjects seem jejune, trivial, unworthy of the attention of those who seek some larger vision of life in art. Others see Ibsen as following the only course he could in a world no longer ruled by great families, by aristocracy, a world no longer greater than the life audiences were willing to recognize and accept. And yet these others see no less heroism, no less courage in the struggle of men and women to triumph over societal norms, to achieve some kind of fulfillment as individuals in a world where conformity frustrates creativity. Ibsen, says Harold Clurman, saw the vital holiness and beauty of the Christian saints eroded and nearly destroyed by middle-class capitalism. "The 'new truth' which was no longer true for Ibsen included the rationales of science, government, democracy and even art as understood and practiced under capitalism. In relation to these he was as he often has been called an 'anarchist,' though others, more perceptive, sensed the 'aristocrat' in him. Remember his

65

inscription in a friend's album: 'The absolute imperative task of democracy is to make itself aristocratic.'"[2]

We take *A Doll's House* as our premier example. Here we find the classic Ibsen scenario—Nora Helmer, a warm, energetic, bustling young woman, returns to her archetypal middle-class home and her equally archetypal middle-class husband, Torvald, a bank-manager on the make.[3] Helmer has done all the right things—found a proper post, a proper home, and—above all—a proper wife, a wife, at least on the surface, submissive, respectful, pleasant, someone he can show off as one of his prize possessions. He presides over this household, and a bit of the exchange between husband and wife as she returns from a mild pre-Christmas shopping spree suggests the nature of their relationship. Ensconced in his study as Nora returns, Torvald asks, "Is that my little lark twittering out there?" A dutiful Nora tells of her shopping only to hear, "Bought, did you say? All these things? Has my little spend-thrift been wasting money again?" Nora's protestations mean little to this martinet: "Yes, but Torvald, this year we really can let ourselves go a little. This is the first Christmas that we have not needed to economise." Torvald's new post and higher salary notwithstanding, he pompously rules: "That is like a woman! But seriously, Nora, you know what I think about that. No debt, no borrowing. There can be no freedom or beauty about a home life that depends on borrowing and debt." Nora's reply—we wonder about its tone—seems proper and dutiful: "As you please, Torvald," and she receives with childlike gratitude her allotment from her husband.

On the surface we have a highly conventional middle-class marriage, one rooted in appearance, not reality. Below the surface, however, there are early in the play the faintest rumblings in the doll's house. The arrival of Nora's old friend Kristine Linde—widowed, alone and fending for herself in the world—obviously touches Nora. She is mildly annoyed as Kristine compares her own lifestyle—sewing for her mother—with the security of Nora's. When Nora volunteers to intercede with Torvald for a position at the Mutual Bank, Kristine replies with a grateful but patronizing, "How kind you are, Nora, to be so anxious to help me! It is doubly kind in you, for you know so little of the burdens and troubles of life." To which Nora,

66

supposedly the perfect wife, the submissive doll, with a toss of the head answers: "You are just like the others. They all think that I am incapable of anything really serious . . . ." As the exchange continues, Nora reveals the great secret on which the play turns, the secret that points up the courage she has demonstrated in virtually saving Torvald's life when he was ill and needed the warmth of Italy for a cure. But this is only part of the truth, for the real situation is revealed as Krogstad, an old admirer of Kristine, enters. He is the ultimate key to Nora's secret, disgraced by his dismissal from Torvald's bank and now pleading with Nora to intercede for him with her husband. When she explains that she can't, he threatens to expose her— that he had in fact lent her the money for Torvald's Italian trip, and that he knew she had forged her recently deceased father's signature on the promissory note.

Torvald will not hear of restoring Krogstad's post, and, in spite of Nora's brave pleading, Krogstad drops his blackmail letter in the Helmer mailbox. At the evening costume ball Nora dances in a frenzy, according to Helmer "as if your life depended on it," employs every technique of delay to prevent Torvald from reading the letter. Meanwhile Kristine and Krogstad have renewed their acquaintance and fallen in love, and the villain of the piece, eager to rehabilitate himself, writes a second letter, this one touched by repentance and a desire to save Nora.

Torvald, still the soul of respectability, reads Krogstad's blackmail letter in spite of Nora's feverish attempts to distract him. He berates Nora in spite of the sacrifices she made for him; he is totally self-centered in his reactions.

> Now you have destroyed all my happiness. You have ruined all my future. It is horrible to think of! I am in the power of an unscrupulous man; he can do what he likes with me, ask anything he likes of me, give me any orders he pleases—I dare not refuse. And I must sink to such miserable depths because of a thoughtless woman!

The action moves quickly to the great climax as Krogstad's letter of apology to Nora is intercepted by Torvald. The ultimate hypocrisy is revealed as Torvald is thrilled by the withdrawal of the threat of exposure. "Nora!" he says, ". . . No, I must read it

once again . . . . Yes, it is true! I am saved! Nora, I am saved!''
Nora's gathering courage, her emerging sense of her self and of
her husband's selfishness, her recognition of the ultimate folly
of their supposed marriage is caught in her simple question
"And I?''

There is no stopping the tragedy now, no stopping Nora's
assertion of herself, of her need to be free, to face the darkness
in order to find the light. Like the heroes and heroines of classical tragedy, she is willing to sacrifice everything—home,
husband, children—to discover the reality albeit the reality is a
different one from Oedipus', Antigone's, Hamlet's, Lear's. The
reality is society, a mechanized, frustrating force that inhibits
individual expression, that demands conformity to secure
respectability. The tragic flaw is not in the fates; the vicious
mole is not within. Society is the culprit.

The dramatic interaction that closes the play is memorable,
Nora resolutely outlining her plan to leave home and family,
Torvald unable to understand anything of what has happened.
His words to Nora reveal that he has learned nothing. She "had
not sufficient knowledge of the means she used." She must
"lean on me; I will advise you and direct you." "I have forgiven
you, Nora." As she prepares to leave the room, she replies
sarcastically, "Thank you for your forgiveness."

The denouement and closing of the play is intense, especially
Nora's words that capture so vividly the issue of the play—the
individual's, the individual woman's need to discover the truth,
especially the truth about herself, to cut through the sham of
society, the false values to discover a core of reality, a core to
live by. It is powerful dialogue, Nora pressing her reasons for
leaving everything, Torvald relentlessly but futilely pursuing
conventional rhetoric for home, family, marriage. But the
dialogue only widens the gap, underlines Nora's image of the
eight-year marriage as not a marriage at all, Torvald's inability to
understand the nature of women, their need to express, communicate, love deeply. The ball is over; husband and wife
prepare for bed, but Nora resolves—now in an everyday dress—
that she "shall not sleep tonight." Torvald—disappointed—
cannot understand, attributes her restlessness to the verve of
her tarentella dancing.

And so the encounter intensifies as husband and wife—perhaps a gentle anticipation of the later great husband and wife encounter of George and Martha in Albee's *Who's Afraid of Virginia Woolf?*—talk to each other. But the talk, as Nora is quick to note, is different: "We have been married eight years. Does it not occur to you that this is the first time that we two, you and I, husband and wife, have had a serious conversation?" Torvald cannot understand, condescendingly questioning, "Was it likely that I would be continually and forever telling you about worries that you could not help me to bear?" Not worries, Nora replies, "I say that we have never sat down in earnest together to try and get to the bottom of anything." And —with withering criticism of the men in her life: "That is just it; you have never understood me. I have been greatly wronged, Torvald—first by papa and then by you." Torvald, like Willy Loman to Biff later, can only reply with stock charges like "unreasonable" and "ungrateful."

She will leave; she puts it as abruptly and as definitively as possible. Respectability-oriented as always, Torvald responds automatically, "To desert your home, your husband, your children! And you don't consider what people will say!" What about her role; what about what society expects? "I don't believe that any longer," says Nora. "I believe that before all else I am a reasonable human being, just as you are—or, at all events, that I must try and become one." In spite of her background and Torvald's chidings, she doesn't "exactly know what religion is." She "is going to see if I can make out who is right, the world or I."

The memory of Torvald's response to Krogstad's letters, his self-concern, his failure to be supportive and loving, made her realize, "I had been living here with a strange man, and had borne him three children . . . . Oh, I can't bear to think of it! I could tear myself into little bits!"

Torvald's pleas are to no avail; Nora releases him from all obligation. Picking up her luggage, heading for Kristine's, she answers his question about a reconciliation. "Ah, Torvald, the most wonderful thing of all would have to happen." Torvald stands alone—in his tracks—with a sudden hope, but with a question that he cannot possibly answer—"The most wonderful thing of all . . . ?" And the door below slams shut.

It is a powerful ending, a tragic one, we are tempted to say, although, as already suggested, not one culminating in epic struggles and deaths of Antigone or Oedipus or Hamlet or Lear. But is it any less poignant? The cloud of a new conformity has shrouded a world, and men and women, like the man and woman on Matthew Arnold's "darkling plain," are conditioned by it. They find older values challenged, at times wanting. Yet Nora Helmer would break out, would sacrifice everything to discover who she is, perhaps a wife, a mother, but certainly a better woman. She has, in the true spirit of classical tragedy, come to terms with her essentially human nature. There has been great disruption, sadness, and loss as Nora faces the darkness, but there is a new realization of the possibilities of greatness of spirit in the ordinary human being.

A Doll's House is, of course, only one of Ibsen's plays, but it is in so many ways representative of his problem tragedy. We might also consider two of his other plays in this genre, less intensively perhaps but with a view to pointing up his central concerns. *Ghosts,* written two years later with its heroine Helen Alving at the center of things, is a denser, more symbolic play, indeed a more shocking play for its time with its use of venereal disease as a key element in the plot, with its references to cohabitation, incest. It has, however, the dimension of tragedy, disaster meeting a good, although quite ordinary, woman, disaster not rooted in her but in the ghosts of her past, of a society that trapped her and her son Osvald in the darkness of loss.

The return of Osvald from Paris, where he has been since he was seven, sets things in motion. In him Mrs. Alving, a widow for ten years, unable to fulfill worthy dreams, sees some hope of a future. She has been enveloped in a world of self-indulgence and sham: the lust of a respectable husband, and the secret of his venereal disease; his fathering of a child by a maidservant, daughter of a neighboring carpenter; the greed and unscrupulousness of Engstrand planning to set up a brothel euphemistically called a Seaman's Home; the religious hypocrisy of a Pastor Manders who had practically forced Mrs. Alving back into a marriage she was ready to abandon, and who had allowed himself to be bribed by Engstrand; the lust of Osvald and Regina; the ultimate doom of her son.

Her son's return, then, seems like a chance for a new begin-

70

ning, a light in the midst of the dank rains that envelop the play. She will live through him and his creativity and art, will blot out the unhappy memories of her hypocritical husband. "No; and then this long dreadful comedy will be at an end. After to-morrow I shall feel as if my dead husband had never lived in this house. There will be no one else here then but my boy and his mother." What a shocking moment as they both hear from the dining room Osvald making advances on Regina. Manders does not understand the horror as Mrs. Alving—with memories of the past and omens of the future—cries, "Ghosts! The couple in the conservatory—over again." The horror! A dream shattered! Honesty overcome by deceit! The sins of the parents visited on the children!

When Osvald plans to marry Regina who yearns for the delights of Paris, Mrs. Alving resolves that she must reveal her secret to both. Already Osvald has complained of a weakness that has sapped his creativity. Manders, concerned as always with appearances, counsels silence: "You have built up a happy illusion in your son's mind, Mrs. Alving—and that is a thing you certainly ought not to undervalue." But she will have none of this duplicity, and actually blames Manders—her representative of the hypocrisy of organized religion—for her past dishonesty:

> Yes, by forcing me to submit to what you called my duty and my obligations; by praising as right and just what my soul revolted against, as it would against something abominable. That was what led me to examine your teach-ings critically. I only wanted to unravel one point in them; but as soon as I had got that unravelled, the whole fabric came to pieces. And then I realized that it was only machine-made.

Mrs. Alving sees in the relationship of Osvald and Regina "Ghosts." "It is," she says, "not only what we have inherited from our fathers and mothers that exists again in us, but all sorts of old dead ideas and all kinds of old dead beliefs and things of that kind." She sees and feels "ghosts all over the world . . . . And we are so miserably afraid of the light, all of us."

Yet the ghosts will not go away. Engstrand, knowing Manders better than Manders knows himself, persuades him that he had been responsible for the catastrophic fire at the orphanage, and then agrees to take the blame in exchange for help in building his so-called Seaman's Home. Once again blackmail is the order of the day in Ibsen's world of appearances.

The climax of the tragedy comes quickly as Regina and Osvald learn the truth about his father, that they are, in fact, half-brother and sister. Regina quickly becomes part of her father's scheme, and Osvald, weaker and weaker, plots suicide. Mother and son talk through the night until sunshine ironically breaks through the darkness. He begs his shocked mother to aid in his plan, but she pleads, tries to prevent him, "I, who gave you life!" only to be stunned by his "I never asked you for life. And what kind of a life was it that you gave me? I don't want it. You shall take it back." We are left with the spectacle of a distraught Mrs. Alving—alone with a dying son, dreams collapsed, the sun rising to Osvald's command—crying, "I can't bear it!"

Hedda Gabler is in a sense a bridge between the problem plays and the more psychologically oriented, symbolic problem plays of the last years. Hedda, a strikingly aristocratic woman with high romantic aspirations, has, to the bewilderment of all, married the pedantic George Tessman, a scholar of sorts who finds his pleasure in editing other writers' manuscripts. A wimpy, fastidious, cautious man, he seems like the most unlikely husband for Hedda. As the play opens, they have returned from an extended wedding trip that has convinced Hedda of the wrongness of her decision to marry for security. Even George's hope for the professorship he sought, which would have brought the luxuries she craved, seems threatened by the free-spirited, creative but erratic and vulnerable Eilert Lovburg, recent author of a wide-ranging and brilliant history of civilization. Eilert's creativity is everything that Tessman is not, and the news that the devoted, protective Thea Elvsted has become a guide to Lovburg's work, the woman behind the man, increased Hedda's frustration. She is the classic world-weary heroine of modernist literature, trapped in a boring world, having lost her early passionate love and now finding her chief pleasure in the pistols left to her by her father, General Gabler. How to perform one great gesture, even a destructive one? How to control one human destiny? The occasion quickly arises. Lovburg arrives at the Tessman's home, and is whisked off for a social evening by Tessman and Judge Brack, a dapper, prideful, conniving former rejected suitor of Hedda. A wild party ensues, so reports George on his early return home, and Lovburg carouses, visits the establishment of Madamoiselle Diana, and in the process loses his precious manuscript, a loss he confesses to Hedda.

Faithful George has found the manuscript, brought it home, and Hedda, in an act that rings with symbolism, burns it. As she throws the manuscript into the fire, she whispers to herself: "Now I am burning your child, Thea!—Burning it, curly-locks. Your child and Eilert Lovburg's. I am burning—I am burning your child." Lovburg is beside himself, saddened that his book is gone, a book with so much of Thea's devotion in it. He will do away with himself, and Hedda, with a maniacal enthusiasm, encourages him, "Eilert Lovburg—listen to me.—Will you not try to—to do it beautifully?" A smiling Lovburg replies, "Beautifully? With vine-leaves in my hair, as you used to dream in the old days . . . ?" But a jaded, obsessed Hedda replies, "No, no. I have lost my faith in the vine-leaves. But beautifully nevertheless! For once in a way!—Goodbye! You must go now—and do not come here any more."

The final indignity is Judge Brack's discovery of the source of the pistol that unromantically killed Lovburg and his blackmailing of Hedda who shockingly puts a bullet through her head, ignominious deaths far from her exuberant dreams and plans. "So I am in your power, Judge Brack," she says to a gloating Judge Brack who savors the prospect of Hedda as his mistress. "A slave, a slave then!" she continues. 'No, I cannot endure the thought of that! Never!" And she will not. She will leave an unromantic world, a world where creativity cannot prosper, long-haired Thea piecing together, pedantic George editing a manuscript based on Lovburg's notes for his book, Judge Brack wooing her to his heart's content. Hedda, trapped, fondles her pistols, with the ridiculous George crying "Fancy that!" and the cynical, incredulous Judge Brack, shouting, "Good God!—people don't do such things."

Tragedy, we say? We certainly need a wider view if we are to deal with the question posed at the beginning and during the course of these lectures. Ibsen's world, as we have been noting, is smaller, more confined, in some ways claustrophobic. His heroes and heroines are smaller in status and stature, but can we easily concede that they are smaller in spirit? We ask the question, and we are of two minds at least. We look back and see some of the signs of Antigone or Hamlet. We look ahead and perhaps see anticipations of Willy Loman, the Tyrones. George Bernard Shaw in his classic *The Quintessence of Ibsenism* is a pioneer in speaking well of Ibsen, in giving tragic status to his drama:

> Ibsen saw that, on the contrary, the more familiar the situation, the more interesting the play. Shakespeare had put ourselves on the stage but not our situations. Our uncles seldom murder our fathers, and cannot legally marry our mothers . . . Ibsen supplies the want left by Shakespeare. He gives us not only ourselves, but ourselves in our situations. The things that happen to his stage figures are things that happen to us. One consequence is that his plays are much more important to us than Shakespeare's. Another is that they are capable both of hurting us cruelly and of filling us with excited hopes of escape from idealistic tyrannies, and with visions of intenser life in the future.[4]

Strong claims for Ibsen, brave prophecies for the enduring qualities of his plays. At any rate we must pay attention to such words, to keep attending to the persistence of a literary form that important critics continue to call tragedy.

NOTES

1. In *A Krutch Onmibus: Forty Years of Social and Literary Criticism* (New York: William Morrow and Co., Inc., 1970), pp. 42-45.

2. *Ibsen* (New York: Macmillan Publishing Co., Inc., 1977), p. 199.

3. The translations of Ibsen in this chapter are from *Eleven Plays of Henrik Ibsen,* introduction by H.L. Mencken (New York: Modern Library, N.D.).

4. (New York: Hill and Wang, 1957), p. 182.

CHAPTER 4

Eugene O'Neill and The Search for an American Tragedy

> "None of us can help the things life has done to us. They're done before you realize it, and once they're done they make you do other things until at last everything comes between you and what you'd like to be, and you've lost your true self forever."
>
> *Long Day's Journey Into Night*

W E make another leap in our investigation of episodes in the history of tragedy. Again time and space are the enemies in a series of lectures like these because so much must be omitted. We must bypass fertile and provocative plays like George Bernard Shaw's *Saint Joan* and T.S. Eliot's *Murder in the Cathedral* with their noble hero and heroine challenging the political and religious establishment in the name of conscience and duty, suffering death in the process, but always with the assurance of a divine reward beyond death. Both plays raise the key question implied throughout these discussions. Are true tragedy and the consolation of religion compatible? Is the promise of a divine bliss after earthly suffering too strong a guarantee for tragic heroism, for the kind of boundary-line situation—described by Murray Krieger and others—where the hero or heroine—with no hope of a divine payoff—stands alone, challenges the unknown, risks everything to assert the claims of the self![1] And we must also bypass the great Irish drama of Synge and O'Casey with their stark, wonderfully lively portrayals of people who live close to the soil, experience the large emotions of love, patriotism, despair, who suffer and yet endure.

But enough for apologies. Clearly the next great episode takes us to America, to a remarkable creative outburst beginning with the emergence of Eugene O'Neill in the 1920's and moving to the plays of Arthur Miller and Tennessee Williams in the 1940's and 1950's especially, to a host of others. And as we make this transition, we need, however briefly, to remind ourselves of the theme of our last lecture, that with Ibsen there is the passing of a certain kind of aristocratic heroism, a deeper concern with the possibilities of greatness in seemingly lesser mortals. The problem we face in American as well as British and Continental "tragedy"—if we may use the term in advance of discussing it—is the seemingly complete disappearance of largeness in the characters, at least largeness in the sense of status and values. We face the derelicts of O'Neills' *Iceman Cometh,* the emotionally ravaged children of Williams, the dreamers of Miller, the demythologized J.B. of Archibald Macleish, the desolate, abandoned bums of Beckett, yes even the foul-mouthed, sleazy war-veterans and used-care salesmen of David Rabe and David Mamet. It is a problem not easily faced, yet one that must be faced as long as we continue to use the word tragedy to describe them.

One interesting way of introducing the problem is to focus immediately on Eugene O'Neill, perhaps our greatest playwright, and on a celebrated review of his *The Iceman Cometh,* one of the two plays to be considered in our lecture. The time is 1946; twelve years of silence have followed the early plays; the horror of World War II has, after a fashion, passed. The editorialist in *Life* magazine, December 2, 1946, dislikes the play, but, more interesting, he sees it as the end of the era of tragic drama. He further argues that democracy, with all its special blessings, is at the root of the failure, and that we must moderate our democratic faith if we want writers of the caliber of Sophocles, Shakespeare, or even Ibsen. No first-rate tragedy has emerged in America despite the tragic events that surround us. The characters of *The Iceman Cometh,* he contends, "are miserable specimins indeed." Instead of the ennobling effect produced by tragedy of the first order, the effect of *The Iceman Cometh* is more like that of a "cosmic bellyache." Audiences in Athens and Shakespeare's England "were able to suffer vicariously with their tragic heroes in an emotional workout that left them wiser and more serene." Their plays were what Aristotle had in mind

76

when he spoke of the ultimate purpose of tragedy—to purge the emotions through pity and fear. But, he says, "Americans disapprove of fear and want to free the world of it. Are we an essentially untragic people?" The American stage makes us feel comfortable with equals or inferiors. "The *Iceman* carries this democratic snobbism about as far as it can be carried; the characters all start out as a bunch of drunken bums and finish the same."

The review closes on a note of faint hope—that we Americans must recover our awareness of evil, our sense of fear, must envision man's "occasional greatness" instead of talking about the stature of the common man. "For tragedy, in essence, is the spectacle of a great man confronting his own finiteness and being punished for letting his reach exceed his grasp." We must likewise qualify our faith in unlimited progress, must recover "the old convictions on which tragedy depends, that man is finite (or sinful) and that his destiny does not lie wholly in his own hands."

Somber words indeed given the date, and even more somber for us who have watched the progress or regression of events from the time of the *Life* magazine editorial and the spirit abroad in the world as we deliver these lectures. It would be too pious, too glib to dismiss those words and to hope for a new Oedipus or King Lear or even a Nora Helmer. For we have moved beyond kingship, beyond aristocracy, the picture of great men and women singlehandedly taking up arms against the evils that beset them. In spite of its great blessings, egalitarianism has taken its toll. We tend not to look up but around us at kindred or lesser spirits. Our sense of heroism has been eroded, and we feel a sense of hopelessness as mechanization threatens the uniqueness of the individual and nuclear madness threatens not just the idea of progress, but the very survival of the planet and its inhabitants.

And yet art goes on in spite of literary and cultural criticism. Eugene O'Neill, considered by many as "The Father of American Tragedy," although he could hardly see our future, saw its beginnings with clarity and intensity of feeling. He looked around and saw no "heroes," but only ordinary men and women—how often they seem to be himself and his family— caught in a forbidding world and yet struggling not so much

77

with mind as with raw physical instinct. They appear trapped by a past over which they have no control and by the dream of a future they will never realize, loving and hating, but always enduring.

Born on Broadway on October 16, 1888, O'Neill knew the theater from his earliest days. The son of James O'Neill—the prototype of James Tyrone in *Long Day's Journey Into Night*—he toured with the family, moving from one boarding school to another. Like so many of his predecessors in the world of writing, while he was unsuccessful in the formal academic process, he read voraciously—his plays often suggest a bibliography—in Balzac, Zola, Wilde, Swinburne, Dowson, Kipling, Ibsen, Shaw, Nietzsche, many others. When not viewing one of his father's innumerable performances as *The Count of Monte Cristo,* he attended the theater to see Ibsen, Yeats, Synge. How he loved the sea—the New London home near the waterfront; living on Cape Cod; in Bermuda; at Sea Island, Georgia; at Marblehead, Massachusetts.

O'Neill married Kathleen Jenkins in 1909, fathered a child Eugene Jr., and shipped out in search of gold in Honduras, and later in Buenos Aires and South Africa. Divorced in 1912, he later spent five months at Gaylord Farm, Connecticut where he was treated for tuberculosis and where he read widely—especially Strindberg and Nietzsche—and resolved to become a playwright. At Gaylord he began to write regularly and produced a series of one-act plays—*Bound East for Cardiff* stands out—and, like so many young aspiring playwrights of the time, attended the celebrated Drama Workshop of Professor George Pierce Baker at Harvard in 1913-1914. From Harvard he went to Greenwich Village, with its colorful colony of artists and radicals, then on to Cape Cod in 1916 where he became associated with the Provincetown Players which performed his *Bound East for Cardiff.* A second marriage in 1918 to Agnes Boulton produced two children, Shane and Oona, and ended in divorce and the disowning of the children.

From one-act plays to full-length dramas, O'Neill's career exploded despite deep personal tragedy, the death of his father James in 1920, of his drug-addicted mother Mary in 1922, and of his alcoholic brother Jamie in 1923. *Beyond the Horizon* won him a Pulitzer Prize in 1920 as did *Anna Christie* in 1922,

Strange Interlude in 1928, and later *Long Day's Journey Into Night* in 1957. In 1937 he won the Nobel Prize for literature. There are, of course, many plays beyond the prize-winners— the expressionistic *The Emperor Jones* and *The Hairy Ape* of 1920-1921, *Desire Under the Elms* (1924) with its mood of Greek tragedy, the experimental *The Great God Brown* (1925) with its intriguing use of masks, *Strange Interlude* (1927) with its Joycean interior monologues.

O'Neill's last marriage, to the actress Carlotta Monterey, forever remembered by O'Neill's dedication of *Long Day's Journey Into Night* to her as "a tribute to your love and tenderness which gave me the faith in love to face my dead at last," brought him a peace that seemed to trigger even greater creativity. There is the ambitious *Mourning Becomes Electra* (1929-1931), his massive American rendering of the Aeschylean *Oresteia* trilogy, the more gentle, nostalgic *Ah, Wilderness* (1933). The period from 1935-1945 is one of quiet, at least for the publication of new plays. We know that he is at work on a master cycle of history plays that will follow America from the Revolution to the Great Depression—*A Tale of Possessors Self-Dispossessed*—although only *A Touch of the Poet* and *More Stately Mansions* have survived.

With the production of *The Iceman Cometh* in 1946 followed by *A Moon for the Misbegotten* in 1947 and *Long Day's Journey Into Night* in 1956, O'Neill once again captures the attention of audiences, critics, and scholars. His last ten years had been painful both physically and emotionally. A palsy-like disease had made writing difficult as early as the 1930's and finally, in spite of a mind alive and alert, made it impossible. He died— within a stone's throw of this lecture hall—in a Boston hotel room on November 27, 1953.

Like O'Neill or not—and few have had stronger advocates and detractors—he was a towering figure in American drama for three decades, and his plays, in revivals, movies, and television productions, continue to have great vitality. Clearly like his heroes Ibsen and Strindberg he broke with conventions of all kinds. He carried Ibsen's concern with common men and women to the limit. We now see on the stage alcoholics, drug-addicts, washed up actors, torn families vividly dramatized in their struggle to exist and survive. There is a new and powerful earthiness to his language and dialogue. A realist to be sure, he is, from early plays to late, interested in all kinds of expressionistic techniques, bringing to the stage masks, puppets, dreams, rapidly shifting scenes, and the like. His use of Greek mythology, his plan to do a series of plays chronicling his vision of American society—these represented major experiments.

And yet pioneer though he was, O'Neill will be remembered not so much for his technical prowess, but for his attempt at something like modern tragedy dramatizing the struggle of lesser mortals to battle with their fate, their environment, with themselves even when illusion seems the only answer. And it is this attempt that concerns us in these lectures on the persistence of tragedy. Critical assessment of the results has varied, of course. For every sharply critical attack—witness that of the reviewer in the *Times Literary Supplement* for April 10, 1948— on his philosophy as a "mass of undisciplined emotions and jejune opinions," and his world as "a dirty pub, frequented by drunks and disorderlies and shiftless loafers . . . a bestiary full of vulpine animals and crushed worms,"[2] there are two or three eloquent tributes like that of Joseph Wood Krutch. For Krutch "true tragedy may be defined as a dramatic work in which the outward failure of the principal personage is compensated for by the dignity and greatness of his character." O'Neill has something of this spirit in his plays:

> Unlike the plays of "literary" playwrights, his dramas have nothing archaic about them. They do not seek the support of a poetic faith in any of the conceptions which served the classical dramatists but are no longer valid for us. They are, on the contrary, almost cynically "modern" in their acceptance of a rationalistic view of man and the universe. Yet he has created his characters upon so large a scale that their downfall is made once more to seem not merely pathetic, but terrible.[3]

We will, as in earlier lectures, not attempt a survey of such an extraordinary dramatic career or a final judgment of O'Neill's ultimate success or failure as a tragedian. But we will focus on two major and representative plays—*The Iceman Cometh* and *Long Day's Journey Into Night*—and explore the continuing description of these plays as part of a tradition of tragedy.[4]

The Iceman Cometh is certainly one of the ultimate tests for tragedy. Here in the most constricted and unheroic of settings—Harry Hope's bar, the Utopia of Illusion—are gathered the dregs of the earth, wounded almost unalterably by the vagaries of their lives, unable to try again, taking comfort in pipe dreams and the security of the bottle. We have Harry Hope himself, proprietor, with his dream of returning to ward politics; Willie Oban, the proud Harvard Law School alumnus; Hugo Kalmar, former editor of radical, anarchist periodicals; Mosher and McGloin, one a former circus-man, the other a former police-lieutenant; Piet Wetjoen and Cecil Lewis, veterans and nostalgists of the Boer War; Joe Mott, a Black man who once owned a thriving gambling house; Jimmy Tomorrow; and others.

And then there is Larry Slade, O'Neill's mouthpiece we suppose, once an anarchist newspaperman. They are a sorry lot as they huddle together in the back room, berating each other, fearing the light of the outside world. Larry calls them "fellow inmates." "They've all a touching credulity concerning tomorrows." He is supposedly, as the bartender Rocky calls him, "De old Foolosopher" with no pipe dreams. "Mine," says Larry, "are all dead and buried behind me. What's before me is the comforting fact that death is a fine long sleep, and I'm damned tired, and it can't come too soon for me." His alliance with anarchism, he claims, is over: "And I took a sleep in the grandstand of philosophical detachment to fall alseep observing the cannibals do their death dance." Hugo spouts his standard radical rhetoric—"Capitalist swine! Bourgeois stoolpigeons!" They are, of course, waiting for one Theodore Hickman or the Iceman as he is popularly known, a salesman. Larry needs Hickman as much as he needs alcohol. What keeps him from going to sleep, he tells Rocky, is "not so much the hope of booze, if you can believe that. I've got the blues and Hickey's a great one to make a joke of everything and cheer you up." Here also is a key character, Don Parritt, a former West Coast anarchist disillusioned with the movement and especially with his radical mother, a tyrannical promiscuous woman and a former lover of Larry, whom Parritt betrayed to the police.

The play moves slowly, revealing the secret of Parritt's betrayal of his mother not for money, but out of hatred. "I think that's why she still respects you, because it was you who left her . . . She just had to keep on having lovers to prove to herself how free she was . . . It made home a lousy place." Also revealed is Parritt's hatred of the Iceman—"I hate his guts! I don't want anything to do with him! I'm scared of him, honest. There's something not human behind his damned grinning and kidding" —and Larry's agreement—"Ah, you feel that, too?"

Alas, Hickey, the purveyor of pipe dreams, arrives, jovial, demonstrative. "Bejees, Hickey, you old bastard, it's good to see you!" shouts Harry Hope. "Here's your key, Hickey. Same old room," Rocky the bartender welcomes him. But there is a change. Hickey is "through with the stuff." "I finally had the guts to face myself and throw overboard the damned lying pipe dream that's been making me miserable and do what I had to do for the happiness of all concerned—and then all at once I found I was at peace with myself and I didn't need booze anymore. That's all there was to it." He's at Hope's bar on a mission, not to save them from alcohol but from "pipe dreams. I know now from my experience, they're the things that really poison and ruin a guy's life and keep him from finding any peace."

Slowly what seems to be a formless ensemble piece reveals a shape, as Hickey and Parritt, revolving around Larry, reach some kind of revelation. Hickey's arrival—the Iceman of Death —has for a time roused the inmates of Hope's bar, especially Hope himself, who resolves to collect himself and face the world again. Drinks for all, says Hickey. Down with the cynicism of Larry. There's hope and love if pipe dreams are abolished. "Here's the toast, Ladies and Gents! Here's to Harry Hope, who's been a friend in need to every one of us." This is no foolish toast, he assures Harry and the assembled group at a Last Supper setting. "And I mean it when I say I hope today will be the biggest day in your life, and in the lives of everyone here, the beginning of a new life of peace and contentment where no pipe dreams can ever nag at you again."

How ironical that Hickey has lived with his own pipe dream, revealing ultimately that he killed his wife Evelyn not out of love, but hatred, hatred that she loved him in his worthlessness. The great revelation speech:

> The one possible way to make up to her for all I'd made her go through, and get her rid of me so I couldn't make her suffer any more, and she wouldn't have to forgive me again! I saw I couldn't do it by killing myself, like I wanted to for a long time. That would have been the last straw for her. She'd have died of a broken heart to think I could do that to her . . . But as it was, there was only one possible way . . . I had to kill her.

A stunned crowd hears Hickey's confession as he prepares for arrest. Larry chides this new Hickey with "We may hate you for what you've done here this time, but we remember the old times, too, when you brought kindness and laughter with you instead of death. We don't want to know things that will make us help send you to the Chair!" Yet Hickey's confession moves Parritt to make his own confession, "I may as well confess, Larry. There's no use lying any more. You know, anyway. I didn't give a damn about the money. It was because I hated her." Pained as Hickey is taken away by the police, Larry prays, "May the Chair bring him peace at last, the poor tortured bastard!" and then turns on the contrite Parritt who would associate himself with Hickey and shouts, "Go! Get the hell out of life, God damn you, before I choke it out of you!" Parritt, as the stage directions indicate, is transformed, touches Larry gently and says, "Thanks, Larry. I just wanted to be sure. I can see now it's the only possible way I can ever get free from her."

So much love wasted, so much capacity for goodness wasted. All attempts to leave the bar end in failure; all must return or die. Waste, as many have argued, is part of the fabric of tragedy, a life gone wrong, hatred that might have been love, death that might have been life. Larry seems to speak so vividly for O'Neill at the end. The only hope is in the struggle; the final release is death.

> Ah! the damned pity—the wrong kind, as Hickey said! Be God, there's no hope! I'll never be a success in the grandstand—or anywhere else! Life is too much for me! I'll be a

fool looking with pity at the two sides of everything till the day I die! May that day come soon! Be God, I'm the only real convert to death Hickey made here. From the bottom of my coward's heart I mean that now!

And Hope's voice echoes the feelings of the inhabitants of the Utopia of Illusion—"Hey there, Larry! Come over and get paralyzed! What the hell you doing, sitting there?"

Laurence Langer, in the midst of the varying critical response to *The Iceman Cometh,* may not have made the ultimate critical statement about the tragic dimension of the play, but he certainly advances an observation that provokes all of us who try to see and understand what lies behind the lost souls at Harry Hope's, behind the coming of the Iceman. For Langer there are moments in the play "that suddenly strip the soul of a man stark naked, not in cruelty or moral superiority, but with an understanding compassion which sees him as a victim of the ironies of life and of himself. These moments are for me the depth of tragedy, with nothing more than can be possibly said."[5]

Long Day's Journey Into Night is classic family tragedy, indeed classic O'Neill family tragedy. Seldom has a playwright turned so overtly to his own life, his own family, his own sufferings for the stuff of his drama. Seldom has a playwright, in a dedication to his wife Carlotta, already mentioned in our lecture, given his readers the clues to the world and people of a play, to a purpose for writing that play. "I mean it," as he writes to Carlotta, "as a tribute to your love and tenderness which gave me the faith in love that enabled me to write this play— write it with deep pity and understanding and forgiveness for all the four haunted Tyrones." The play, like *Iceman* of course, was a new kind of tragedy, a new kind of drama, and the responses to its intense subjectivity were wide-ranging. John Chapman (*New York Daily News,* November 8, 1956), while seeing it as "about himself, his parents, and his brother," saw that "the drama could have been written and very possibly was written about anybody else." "As they tell of themselves, each in a long monologue, these people become larger than their own small lives; they become humanity, looking for something but not knowing exactly what it is looking for. They are magnifi-

The haunted Tyrone family in O'Neill's *Long Day's Journey into Night*—
Frederic March as James, Florence Eldridge as Mary, Bradford Dillman as
Edmund and Jason Robards, Jr. as Jamie.

cent."[6] Thomas Dash (*Women's Wear Daily,* November 8, 1956) is less sanguine: "For the *cognoscenti* and for devotees of O'Neill, these flagellations and psychological penetrations into the pitiful ruins of a family may prove stimulating. But for the neutral and dispassionate observer and for the rank and file of theatregoers, "A Long Day's Journey Into Night" may prove a long night's journey without too much daylight."[7]

The time is summer 1812. The place is a summer house near the Connecticut shore, a place of alternating sun and mist and fog. The principals are the Tyrone family—James, a formidable man, an actor of great promise who made a career as a one-play man in the melodramatic *The Count of Monte Cristo;* Mary, a shy, charming, but now emotionally weakened woman who has been seduced by drugs; Jamie, the older son, now thirty-three, a ne'er-do-well cynic, angry at the world and at himself; and Edmund—O'Neill himself perhaps—early twentiesh—sickly, sensitive, with a touch of the poet. The action takes place from early morning to late night of one day, a day of love and tenderness, of hatred and laceration as the family lives in one day a lifetime, a day in which the persisting O'Neill theme of a presentness of the past, the ghosts of other times, other places, the specter of lost hopes persists. The fog has lifted as James and Mary enter the living room after breakfast. Tenderness and tension are both revealed. James is concerned about Mary's poor appetite although pleased that she has gained weight—"I can't tell you the deep happiness it gives me, darling, to see you as you've been since you came back to us, your dear old self again." Mary gently teases James about his snoring like a foghorn. Jamie tries to join in the joking, but tension is obviously building—Tyrone resentful of Jamie's comments and retorting with criticism of Jamie's horseplaying, Mary apprehensive about everyone noticing her seriousness. The mild banter develops with the key word "forget" standing out. Says Mary, "Now James! You musn't be so touchy." Edmund—"Give it a rest, can't you?"; Jamie—"What's all the fuss about? Let's forget it." Tyrone's outburst is the first of many climaxes—"Yes, forget! Forget everything and face nothing! It's a convenient philosophy if you've no ambition in life except to . . . ."

Tyrone's anger is prodded further by Edmund's innocent enough delight in meeting a tenant of Tyrone whose pigs had broken through the fence of Harker, a millionaire, to wallow in the ice-pond. Joking, Edmund says, "I told Shaughnessy he should have reminded Harker that a Standard Oil millionaire ought to welcome the flavor of hog in his ice water as an appropriate touch," and evokes not a laugh but a frowning "The devil you did!" and "Keep your damned Socialist anarchist sentiments out of my affairs!" Again Tyrone, as Mary and the others try to quiet him, shows a tender side, concerned about Edmund's ill health and Doctor Hardy's diagnosis, commenting on how Mary's "eyes are beautiful," her hair "the most beautiful in the world." Yet his pecuniousness, his unwillingness to see the incompetence of Hardy, his shielding of Mary from the knowledge of Edmund's consumption triggers angrier confrontation between father and son—Jamie's "Poor kid!"; Tyrone's vicious, "You dare tell me what I can afford? You've never known the value of a dollar and never will! You've never saved a dollar in your life! At the end of each season you're penniless! You've thrown yourself away every week on whores and whiskey!"; Jamie's "All right, Papa, I'm a bum. Anything you like, so long as it stops the argument." How quickly raging anger can turn to tenderness between father and son. We must help her, says Tyrone. "Of course, Papa," says Jamie, moved. "I'm sorry, Jamie." And back and forth.

Mary is clearly not cured. She has obviously returned to her drug habit, reliving—to the torment of all—her past dreams of being a pianist, a nun. She means to "take advantage of the sunshine before the fog comes back . . . Because I know it will." Enter Edmund sick, discouraged, dreaming of a better world of poetry, beauty, love. Mary would bring him comfort; "All you need is your mother to nurse you. Big as you are, you're still the baby of the family to me, you know." She will also talk of how he and Jamie have disgraced themselves, how she senses her family's suspicion, summing up everything with a characteristic O'Neill candor—"That's what makes it so hard—for all of us. We can't forget."

And so the time moves to mid-day and it now becomes clear that all know of Mary's return to her drug habit. There are further angry exchanges tempered by moments of touching concern for Mary and for Edmund who will finally go with Jamie to Doctor Hardy for some diagnosis of his poor health. Mary, clearsighted in the midst of her darkness, pleads for another doctor, associating Hardy with his incompetent initial prescription of drugs after the difficult birth of Edmund and associating him ultimately with her own addiction:

> Oh, we all realize why you like him, James! Because he's cheap. Heaven knows I ought to after all these years. He's an ignorant fool! There should be a law to keep men like him from practicing. He hasn't the slightest idea—When you're in agony and half insane, he sits and delivers sermons on will power!

She continues with amazing ferocity: "I hate doctors! They'll do anything, anything to keep you coming to them. They'll sell their souls! What's more, they'll sell yours, and you never know until one day you find yourself in hell!" A moment of terror for all—with Edmund's "Mama! For God's sake, stop talking," a shaken James's "Yes, Mary, it's no time," a cynical Jamie's, "Another shot in the arm!" as she leaves the room and heads upstairs. Yet Jamie's choric voice responds sharply but candidly to the criticism of the others: "No pity? I have all the pity in the world for her. I understand what a hard game to beat she's up against—which is more than you ever have!"

Evening comes with dusk and fog, and Mary, alone with the servant girl Cathleen, reminisces about her life, her falling in love, her praying the "Hail Mary." James and Edmund return to a moment of tenderness and love between father and mother. But memories, the past will not go away; she cannot forget his drinking, the loneliness of hotel rooms, the new knowledge of Edmund's fatal illness.

Midnight closes not just the chronological but emotional day for the doomed Tyrones. Darkness, the settling of the fog, the moaning sound of the foghorn—the elements match the mood. A drunken Tyrone, "sad, defeated," plays at cards, lost. Edmund appears, as drunk as his father. Still there are the conflicting emotions. On the one hand, his tender "I'm glad you've come, lad. I've been damned lonely." On the other his angry stinginess—"I told you to turn out that light! We're not giving a ball. There's no reason to have the house ablaze with electricity at this time of night, burning up money." The battle resumes between father and son. Edmund has been walking; his father fears for his condition, says it's not sensible. Edmund—with anger and romance—replies to his father, "To hell with sense! We're all crazy. What do we want with sense?" They play cards, rehearse the past, Edmund complaining about his father's stinginess after his birth, expressing his hatred, James defending himself; Edmund reminding him of his own imminent commitment to the Hilltown Sanatorium, James again complaining about his financial woes.

Tenderness, guilt, remorse return as always. Tyrone rehearses what might have been, his choice of the melodramatic Count of Monte Cristo for money when he might have been a great actor. He recalls Edwin Booth watching him play Othello and praising him as better than himself: "That from Booth, the greatest actor of his day or any other! As I look back on it now, that night was the high spot in my career. I had life where I wanted it! And for a time after that I kept on upward with ambition high. Married your mother . . . But a few years later my good bad luck made me find the big money-maker . . . What the hell was it I wanted to buy, I wonder, that was worth—Well, no matter. It's a late day for regrets." A more understanding Edmund replies, "I'm glad you've told me this, Papa. I know you a lot better now." And Edmund shares his memories, too, especially those at sea— "Then the moment of ecstatic freedom came. The peace, the end of the quest, the last harbor, the joy of belonging to a fulfillment beyond man's lousy, pitiful, greedy fears and hopes and dreams! . . . As it is, I will always be a stranger who never feels at home, who does not really want and is not really wanted, who can never belong, who must always be a little in love with death!"

A drunken Jamie returns—bitter, indignant, hoping to inherit the fortune, angry with his mother, but finally with Edmund— "That's all. Feel better now. Gone to confession. Know you absolve me, don't you, Kid! You understand. You're a damned fine kind kid. Ought to be. I made you. So go and get well. Don't die on me. You're all I've got left. God bless you, Kid." In the midst of all, Mary enters with her wedding gown, and the play is flooded with memory, the past, what might have been. It is O'Neill's most beautiful poetry, a long *apologia pro vita sua,* of how she had told Mother Elizabeth she wanted to be a nun, of how she had to be tested for a year or two. And then, with an indignant toss of the head:

> I never dreamed Holy Mother would give me such advice! I was really shocked. I said, of course, I would do anything she suggested, but I knew it was simply a waste of time. After I left her, I felt all mixed up, so I went to the shrine and prayed to the Blessed Virgin and found peace again because I knew she heard my prayer and would always love me and see no harm ever came to me so long as I never lost my faith in her.

. . . .

> That was in the winter of my senior year. Then in the spring something happened to me. Yes, I remember. I fell in love with James Tyrone and was so happy for a time.

All three stare at her, and the play ends. The journey has been into night, yet ghosts have been exorcised, memories relived, the past felt and understood, and we leave perhaps with some sense of purgation, of lives that turned out differently, but lives lived nevertheless. We truly pity these fellow human beings; we fear their plight; we are wiser; we know something of the essence of human life—its promise, its failures, its fabric. And we are better for it.

From the beginning of our discussion of Ibsen, we have examined the phenomenon of modern tragedy—its movement away from ruling families, great heroes and heroines, of suffering—often unwarranted—faced grandly, of audiences stunned by the greatness of human possibility. We have seen the belief in a universe of order challenged, of the dignity of humankind eroded. We have seen the emergence of the common man and woman in Ibsen, and, in moving to America, in O'Neill. The challenge has been to consider whether, in the modern era, with democratic ideals, demythologizing, the plight of seemingly little men and women can be called tragic. O'Neill summons us to examine closely whether in seeing the terrible waste of great potential, the search for lost dreams, the coming to terms with the reality behind the dream, the wild pursuit of meaning by oftentimes the lowliest of the lowly, we see our situation in universal terms. For some these are indeed lost souls; for others they are souls lost, struggling, surviving, and—in surviving—reminding us of the range of human possibility. If nothing human can be foreign to us, then certainly O'Neill must take his place as an important episode in the history of tragedy. And so too must Arthur Miller and Tennessee Williams, great American playwrights to whom we turn next.

NOTES

1. See Krieger's perceptive observations on this subject in his *The Tragic Vision* (New York: Holt, Rinehart and Winston, 1960), especially the following:

> The tragic vision, a product of crisis and of shock, is an expression of man only in an extreme situation, never in a normal or routine one. Literature dealing with it frequently dwells on the exceptional man; and when it does choose a normal man it does so only to convert him, by way of the extremity he lives through, into the exceptional man. The tragic vision is, by my definition, a vision of extreme cases, a distillate of the rebellion, the godlessness which once induced by crisis, purifies itself by rejecting all palliatives. And the tragic visionary, by the stark austerity of his ontological position in the fable, is the extremist who—despite his rich intermingling with the stuff of experience—finds himself transformed from character to fable. (p. 20)

2. Quoted in Normand Berlin, *Eugene O'Neill* (New York: Grove Press, 1982), pp. 155-156. See also Berlin's powerful tribute to O'Neill as a writer of tragedy: "The celebration of mystery, the pressure of the force behind, the sense of fated frustration and sadness, the nobility of man's struggle or endurance, the dramatization of the question mark of our lives, the knowledge that no answer to life's important questions can ever be found—these are the characteristics of tragedy that allow us to talk of a tragic tradition, of which O'Neill is a powerful representative." (pp. 163-164)

3. *Nine Plays by Eugene O'Neill*. Selected by the Author. Introduction by Joseph Wood Krutch (New York: The Modern Library, 1959), p. xxii.

4. Quotations from the O'Neill plays are from *The Iceman Cometh* (New York: Random House, 1946) and *Long Day's Journey Into Night* (New Haven and London: Yale University Press, 1956).

5. Quoted in Jordan Y. Miller, *Playwright's Progress: O'Neill and the Critics* (Chicago: Scott, Foresman and Company, 1965), pp. 133-134. I am greatly indebted to this remarkable collection and commentary on the critical reviews of O'Neill's plays.

6. Quoted in Miller, p. 136.

CHAPTER 5

Tragedy in Mid-Century America
Tennessee Williams and Arthur Miller

"Nobody dast blame this man. You don't understand: Willy was a salesman. And for a salesman, there is no rock bottom to the life. He don't put a bolt to a nut, he don't tell you the law or give you medicine. He's a man way out there in the blue, riding on a smile and a shoeshine. And when they start not smiling back— that's an earthquake . . . . A salesman is got to dream, boy. It comes with the territory."

Death of a Salesman

"I didn't go to the moon. I went much further —for time is the longest distance between two places—Not long after that I was fired for writing a poem on the lid of a shoe-box. I left St. Louis . . . . Oh Laura, Laura, I tried to leave you behind me, but I am more faithful than I intended to be! I reach for a cigarette, I cross the street, I run into the movies or a bar, I buy a drink, I speak to the nearest stranger—anything that can blow your candles out!—for nowadays the world is lit by lightning! Blow out your candles, Laura—and so goodbye . . . ."

The Glass Menagerie

IF Eugene O'Neill is the father of American tragedy, then clearly Arthur Miller and Tennessee Williams are his major descendants. William Inge, Archibald Macleish, Edward Albee, Peter Schaffer, Eugene Ionesco, Jean Genet, Harold Pinter, Athol Fugard, Marsha Norman, Sam Shepard and other world dramatists notwithstanding, with the exception of Samuel Beckett—to be considered in our final lecture—Williams and Miller have dominated drama in the 1940's and 1950's, and revivals of both—the recent Jessica Tandy *Glass Menagerie,* A People's Republic of China production of a *Death of a Salesman* and the recent Dustin Hoffman portrayal of Willy in New York—continue to be most successful aesthetically and commercially. For they carried the idea of a modern tragedy even further, explored even more deeply the possibility of heroism in the common man or woman, the possibility of an audience being struck by the fate of the father who loves too much, believes too much in the American dream, the lonely, unfulfilled men and women trapped in memories, the survivors of lives of desperation.

ARTHUR MILLER: THE COMMON MAN REVISITED

Arthur Miller is most eloquent in his defense of the tragedy of the common man, his answer to the kind of criticism launched earlier against O'Neill's *Iceman Cometh.* In his celebrated *New York Times* essay of February 27, 1949, he disputes the common wisdom that we are "below tragedy—or tragedy above us. The inevitable conclusion is, of course, that the tragic mode is archaic, fit only for the very highly placed, the kings or the kingly, and where this admission is not made in so many words it is most often implied." The common man is for Miller just as suitable as kings were. "On the face of it this ought to be obvious in the light of modern psychiatry, which bases its analysis upon classic formulations, such as the Oedipus and Orestes complexes, for instance, which were enacted by royal beings, but which apply to everyone in similar emotional situations." In a telling paragraph for all of us who wonder about the stature of a Willy Loman, Tom Wingfield, Blanche Dubois, he argues:

> More simply when the question of tragedy in art is not an issue, we never hesitate to attribute to the well-placed and the exalted the very same mental processes as the lowly. And finally, if the exaltation of tragic action were truly a property of the high-bred character alone, it is inconceivable that the mass of mankind should cherish tragedy above all other forms, let alone be capable of understanding it.

93

What then is the tragic feeling which can be so independent of time? "As a general rule," he argues, "to which there may be exceptions unknown to me, I think the tragic feeling is evoked in us when we are in the presence of a character who is ready to lay down his life, if need be, to secure one thing—his sense of personal dignity." The struggle "is that of the individual attempting to gain his rightful place in his society." Tragedy is "the consequence of a man's total compulsion to evaluate himself justly." The new challenge is the unwillingness to remain passive and the need to take action against "the seemingly stable cosmos around us." In a telling paragraph Miller probes what he regards as the common ground of tragedy:

> The Greeks could probe the very heavenly origin of their ways and return to confirm the rightness of laws. And Job could face God in anger, demanding his right, and end in submission. But for a moment everything is in suspension, nothing is accepted, and in this stretching and tearing apart of the cosmos, in the very action of so doing, the character gains 'size,' the tragic stature which is spuriously attached to the royal or the high born in our minds. The commonest of men may take on that stature to the extent of his willingness to throw all he has into the contest, the battle to secure his rightful place in the world.

Born in New York in 1915 and still alive and active in the overseeing of the several revivals of his plays, Miller graduated from the University of Michigan in 1938 where he studied in the famous Kenneth T. Rowe playwriting class and won several drama writing awards. After graduation he wrote for radio, and more notably, for the Federal Theater Project. He married three times, to Mary Grace Slattery in 1940, to Marilyn Monroe in 1956, and to Inge Morath in 1962. From the time of his first Broadway production, a failed *The Man Who Had All the Luck* in 1944, he dominated the serious New York theater with Pulitzer Prize-New York Drama Critics Circle awards for *All My Sons* in 1947 and *Death of a Salesman* in 1949. During the 1950's he continued an intense preoccupation with social drama in an adaptation of Ibsen's *An Enemy of the People* in 1950 and *The Crucible* in 1953, the latter clearly a McCarthy-era play reflecting Miller's own appearance before the House Un-

94

American Activities Committee. Then followed two compelling one-act plays, *A View from the Bridge* and *A Memory of Two Mondays* (1955); an embarrassingly autobiographical *After the Fall* in 1964 following the breakup of his marriage to Marilyn Monroe; *Incident at Vichy* in 1964 and *The Price* in 1968. His career has, of course, continued with new plays like *The Creation of the World and Other Business* in 1972, but Miller's greatest work is unquestionably the work of the 1940's and 1950's, and his supreme success *Death of a Salesman,* the subject of our lecture tonight, catches what is essential about the man and what, we think, is universal about his work.

To read Miller is to understand the continuing impact of Ibsen on modern drama, not simply the impact of a new common man or a language of everyday life, but of an intense concern with society's impact on the individual, its conditioning of hopes and dreams. As a child of the Great American Depression, Miller as man and artist had come to recognize the need for dramatizing the tension of the individual within society, and it is a key theme in most of the plays although there is a continuing interest in expressionism as technique and the psychological as subject-matter. M.W. Steinberg's comments are illuminating and apt:

Miller's tragedies then tend to fluctuate, often uneasily, between Greek drama with its emphasis on external causes (though Miller tries to avoid its fatalism) and Christian drama, which involves freedom and responsibility and which seeks the source of the tragedy in the individual. His drama is unlike both in that for the most part it rejects a religious framework. Miller, like most modern tragedians, has been seeking a new explanation of the human situation with its tragic aspects. He sees it in naturalistic and humanistic terms, not transcendental ones . . . . Our environment, which restricts and defeats us, which prevents us from realizing ourselves (a failure which to Miller is the heart of the tragic experience) can be changed—if we will . . . the underlying position is optimistic: that man, an object of nature, is more than nature; that Willy Loman, for example, can somehow be more than the force that made him.[1]

Miller's is a man-centered tragedy; his questions, as his stunning essay on tragedy and the common man have already suggested, concern how man is to find his rightful place not hereafter, but now—in this time, this place. Willy Loman is the great archetype, the basically good man, loving wife and sons—perhaps almost too much—loving things natural and beautiful, a person with innate gifts, a dreamer. He is appropriately a salesman, a man selling something, but mostly himself. He is caught in the web of economic society and firmly trapped as a life, a marriage, the raising of sons pass by. How deeply infatuated he becomes with the American dream—appearances over reality, being very well liked, knowing the right people, cutting corners for easy success! What a toll it takes on his ideas of honesty, on love for his wife, on the inculcation of ideas of integrity in his sons Happy and Biff!

Miller strategically introduces us to Willy in one of those boundary-line situations. Whatever heyday he has had is over; he is sixty-two; we learn he is covering the huge New England territory on commission; he is off on another trip, but has unexpectedly returned to his home carrying his two display cases.[2] His wife Linda—who "more than loves him, she admires him" —is surprised even though she has obviously become accustomed to his behaving oddly for some time. From the beginning Willy seems worn-out, frazzled, weak physically, but—more crucial—emotionally. He has had it. He is loving with Linda but sharp in dealing with her questions. With wonder, in a tender moment, he tells Linda of his need to return home:

I was driving along, you understand? And I was fine, I was even observing the scenery. You can imagine me, looking at scenery, on the road every week of my life! But it's so beautiful up there, Linda, the trees are so thick, and the sun is warm. I opened the windshield and just let the warm air bathe over me. And then all of a sudden I'm goin' off the road! I'm tellin' ya, I absolutely forgot I was driving. If I'd've gone the other way over the white line I might've killed somebody. So I went on again—and five minutes later I'm dreamin' again, and I nearly . . . I have such thoughts, I have such strange thoughts.

Thomas Mitchell as Willy Loman in Arthur Miller's *Death of a Salesman*.

Linda, of course, wants him to work in New York in spite of all his protestations about being the "New England man." But Wagner, his old employer, has given way to young son Howard who has reduced Willy to nothing more than a commission salesman despite his great dreams.

The comfort of Linda settles Willy, but only temporarily as they begin to discuss their two sons—one Happy, a ne'er-do-well womanizer, and Biff, Willy's favorite, a one-time football hero taught about success and hating it. Biff is thirty-four, and has been away working as a farmhand. Willy is angry—"Not finding yourself at the age of thirty-four is a disgrace!"—"The trouble is he's lazy, goddammit." Linda intercedes in vain, trying to explain that Biff is lost, but Willy is beyond understanding—"In the greatest country in the world a young man with such personal attractiveness gets lost." With a new sense of pity and determination, he tells Linda: "I'll see him in the morning; I'll have a nice talk with him. I'll get him a job selling. He could be big in no time. My God! Remember how they used to follow him around in high school? When he smiled at one of them their faces lit up!" Willy complains about construction in the neighborhood, then waxes eloquent again. "More and more I think of those days, Linda. This time of year it was lilac and wisteria. And then the peonies would come out, and the daffodils. What fragrance in the room!"

But the dream and the reality are so different. Willy has deteriorated, holds imaginary conversations with an adventurous and successful brother Ben, fantasizes about Biff's football glories, about days of great sales, admiring and yet not admiring his brother Charley, a steady successful businessman, but unlike Willy, "He's liked, but he's not—well liked," about the mistress-secretary in Boston who wields her influence, entertains Willy, the secretary once discovered by Biff in Willy's hotel room when he needed him most. These are powerful fantasies, and they are at the root of Willy's condition. There are moments of illumination about himself with Linda—"But I gotta be at it ten, twelve hours a day. Other men—I don't know —they do it easier. I don't know why—I can't stop myself—I talk too much. A man ought to come in with a few words. One thing about Charley. He's a man of a few words, and they respect him." There's an angry but candid cry to Hap to look at the reality of his situation, "You'll retire me for life on seventy goddam dollars a week? And your women and your car and your apartment, and you'll retire me for life! Christ's sake, I couldn't get past Yonkers today! Where are you guys, where are you? The woods are burning! I can't drive a car!" Yet these moments

98

are brief and faltering; his true self had indeed been lost in the jungle of a dream. And so he cannot accept Charley's offer of a job, cannot recognize Charley's gifts as gifts and instead listens to Ben's, "Opportunity is tremendous in Alaska, William. Surprised you're not up there," to Ben's talk of diamond mines in Africa. What shall I teach my boys, says Willy to Ben. Arrogantly Ben answers: "William, when I walked into the jungle, I was seventeen. When I walked out I was twenty-one. And, by God, I was rich!" Willy enthusiastically replies— "That's just the spirit I want to imbue them with! To walk into the jungle! I was right! I was right! I was right!"

As the boys talk of Willy's condition, and Biff angrily says "He's got no character—Charley wouldn't do this. Not in his own house—spewing out that vomit from his mind," Linda— sounding like Miller himself—defends Willy as tragic and yet worthy of attention. It is a powerful, oft-quoted speech:

> Then make Charley your father, Biff. You can't do that, can you? I don't say he's a great man. Willy Loman never made a lot of money. His name was never in the paper. He's not the finest character that every lived. But he's a human being, and a terrible thing is happening to him. So attention must be paid. He's not to be allowed to fall into his grave like an old dog. Attention, attention must finally be paid to such a person. You called him crazy . . .

In a powerful moment of revelation to her two sons, Linda reveals that Willy has been trying to commit suicide—first by having automobile accidents and then—to the horror of her skeptical sons—by her ultimate discovery in the cellar as she went to fix a fuse box—"And behind the fuse box—it happened to fall out—was a length of rubber pipe—just short."

The boys—half-heartedly—Hap a phony, Biff with his heart elsewhere—resolve to change, to become The Loman Brothers sporting goods outfit, but Willy is captivated, urging Biff on with his philosophy of success, "It's not what you say, it's how you say it—because personality always wins the day," and later, when the boys go off to bed, to Linda "Like a young god. Hercules—something like that. And the sun, the sun all around him. Remember how he waved to me? Right up from the field, with the representatives of three colleges standing by? And the buyers I brought, and the cheers when he came out—Loman, Loman, Loman! God Almighty, he'll be great yet. A star like that, magnificent, can never really fade away." Willy resolves to ask Howard Wagner to work in New York. All seems well.

All seems well, for the past is too much intertwined in the present. Howard rejects Willy's plan, in effect fires him, and Willy returns to Linda with dreams of time gone by, of Biff's success in sports, his flunking of Math despite his cousin Bernard's pleas that he go to Summer School, the Biff trip to New England, Biff's staggering discovery of his father with the secretary in the hotel room.

The boys wait for Willy at a restaurant, for a planned celebration of their new scheme. It is a scene of universal failure, Hap with his women talking big, Willy with the news of his being fired, Biff with his story of disappointment with Oliver, Willy fantasizing about the night in Boston, Biff lovingly but hopelessly telling one of the girls Hap has picked up in the restaurant, "Miss Forsythe, you've just seen a prince walk by. A fine troubled prince. A hard-working unappreciated prince. A pal, you understand? A good companion, always for his boys."

The return home brings the height of the tragedy, the great confrontation scene. All four family members are present, but Biff and Willy are the central figures, reality confronting dream. Indeed many modern critics have argued that Biff is—somewhat ironically—the tragic hero of the play, the character who comes to terms with himself, who discovers the truth about reality, that Willy never learns, that his suicide-plan to bring twenty-thousand dollars to make Biff great and happy is the ultimate illusion of the salesman—"Oh, Ben, that's the whole beauty of it! I see it like a diamond, shining in the dark, hard and rough, that I can pick up and touch in my hand . . . Because he thinks I'm nothing, see, and so he spites me. But the funeral . . . that funeral will be massive . . . I am known, Ben, and he'll see it with his eyes once and for all. He'll see what I am, Ben! He's in for a shock, that boy!" Brian Parker is one such critic dealing with the idea that Willy is a questionable tragic hero because he is deceived to the end. "But," he argues, "the new truth is there in Biff, and the extension of expressionistic technique beyond Willy's death unbroken into the 'Requiem' binds together the two experiences. The extension of the point of view into scenes where Willy does not appear enables the audience at the end to associate Biff's acceptance with Willy's disaster as a single, coherent, and, I would agree, tragic experience."[3]

No more dreams, says Biff, as Willy calls him spiteful, hateful, as Biff confronts him with the rubber tube:

> No! Nobody's hanging himself, Willy! I ran down eleven flights with a pen in my hand today. And suddenly I stopped, you hear me? And in the middle of that office building, do you hear this? I stopped in the middle of that building and I saw—the sky. I saw the things that I love in this world. The work and the food and time to sit and smoke. And I looked at the pen and said to myself, what the hell am I grabbing this for? Why am I trying to become what I don't want to be? What am I doing in an office, making a contemptuous begging fool of myself, when all I want is out there, waiting for me the minute I say I know who I am! Why can't I say that, Willy?

A baffled Willy dreams on, "The door of your life is wide open!" while Biff faces him, "Pop! I'm a dime a dozen, and so are you!" Is this the great man coming to terms with his own mortality? Willy's answer seems almost Lear-like as he turns on Biff furiously with "I am not a dime a dozen! I am Willy Loman and you are Biff Loman." Biff grabs—hungry with love—for Willy, "I'm just what I am, that's all." Momentarily astonished and seemingly recognizing that Biff loved him in spite of everything, Willy muses—"Isn't that—isn't that remarkable? Biff—he likes me!" and "Oh, Biff . . . He cried! Cried to me . . . That boy is going to be magnificent." But Willy is still trapped by the dream—money will bring Biff success, and success will make him happy. The insurance policy means salvation as Willy speeds off to his death in the car.

Nobody comes to Willy's funeral except his family, Linda saying she cannot understand since all he needed was a little salary, the house was free and clear. Biff sees what Willy might have been—"You know something, Charley, there's more to him in that front stoop than in all the sales he ever made." Charley comments: "No man only needs a little salary." Biff says "He never knew who he was." Happy resolves to continue to dream. Charley, leaving Linda alone to wonder, delivers the final requiem:

> Nobody dast blame this man. You don't understand: Willy was a salesman. And for a salesman, there is no rock bottom to the life. He don't put a bolt to a nut, he don't tell you the law or give you medicine. He's a man way out there in the blue, riding on a smile and a shoeshine. And when they start not smiling back—that's an earthquake. And then you get yourself a couple of spots on your hat, and you're finished. Nobody dast blame this man. A salesman is got to dream, boy. It goes with the territory.

Once again the question arises, tragedy or melodrama or something else. Certainly in *Death of a Salesman* or in *All My Sons* we find ordinariness epitomized, and yet there is something of largeness of spirit in a Willy Loman, a Biff Loman. Willy may die of the illusion he was born with, but he dies nevertheless, lays down his life for something he believes in, for a son, for a family. And his breadth of emotion draws us to him; we care; we see waste; we see ourselves capable of the same illusion. No puny Mr. Zero could have this effect; as crowds, we are told, wept night after night at Dustin Hoffman's Willy in New York, there must have been something more than melodrama. Willy must hold out some sense of the possibilities of humankind and the awful and fearsome damage that can be done to those possibilities. Biff may be headed back for a farm in the West, but is it just a farm? Is it a place of light, of awareness, of possibility, a place where Biff Loman can create a life, a world his father dreamed of, but could never create? In the Preface to the first volume of his *Collected Plays,* the volume which includes *Death of a Salesman,* Miller writes of striking a new balance "which embraces both determinism and the paradox of will. If there is one unseen goal toward which every play in this book strives, it is that very discovery and its proof—that we are made and yet more than what made us."[4] He seems to have offered helpful answers to our questions.

TENNESSEE WILLIAMS: THE TRAGIC
AND THE PATHETIC

It may be too glib to associate Tennessee Williams and Eugene O'Neill on the basis of their concern with ordinary men and women who seem victimized not so much by societal pressures, but by ravaged emotional lives, by retreat to a world of illusion for a measure of security. Like O'Neill before him, Williams explores that conflict between illusion and reality. Yet he seems at times to probe the psyche more deeply, to write even more autobiographically, so much so that his characters, whether male or female, seem to be embodiments of himself and the many facets of a complex life. These are people who live in a world of escape, who cannot reach out and touch reality, and if they do, they are destroyed by it. Robert Heilman has noted the O'Neill-Williams kinship, but points up important differences also. "Despite their common interest in characters who collapse or fail, O'Neill and Williams go about the subject differently. O'Neill's people, as we have seen, are self-conscious, striving, attuned to problems and ideas. Williams' people are more given to undefined feeling than to thought, and their troubles originate more often in faulty neurological mechanisms." He further adds, "In Williams' work the sufferers who do not make the grade have an air of illness or something close to it. The early plays deal with hypersensitive characters who, from weakness or disability, either cannot face the world at all or have to opt out of it."[5]

Williams has, of course, been attacked as often as praised for his preoccupation with the insane, the homosexual, the violent, the pathologically weak, the decadent, but, for better or for worse, his plays, like Miller's, dominated the 1940's and 1950's, and revivals of *The Glass Menagerie, A Streetcar Named Desire,* and *Cat on a Hot Tin Roof* have continued regularly over the years. Like him or not, his Blanche Dubois, Stanley Kowalski, the Wingfields, Brick, Big Daddy, and a host of other characters have played vital roles in discussions of the American theater or of American culture. And the word tragedy is constantly used to describe them.

Tennessee—his name was Tom—was born in Columbus,

Mississippi on March 26, 1911; his ancestry was pioneer Tennessee—father a salesman, mother a southern aristocrat, his grandfather an Episcopalian clergyman, characters who find embodiments in several of the plays. The family moved to St. Louis in 1918, and Tom entered the University of Missouri where, more interested in his own writing than in formal study, he did poorly and was forced by his father to take a job at the International Shoe Company Warehouse, a job that offered vivid images of the monotony of routine existence that pervade his plays. He completed his formal education at Washington University in St. Louis and the University of Iowa, receiving a degree from Iowa in 1938. Leaving, or perhaps escaping would be a better word, St. Louis, he travelled the country, working in every kind of job, but very much dedicated to writing, and finally enrolling in John Gassner's playwriting seminar at the New School in New York. An early play *Battle for Angels* failed after being banned in Boston in 1940, and Williams gave Hollywood a try, quitting in disgust at the commercialism of the movie world. 1945 saw the beginning of his great success with *The Glass Menagerie* which opened in Chicago on December 26, 1944 and won him his first New York Drama Critics Circle Award in 1945. *Streetcar Named Desire* won this award plus a Pulitzer Prize in 1947, and a major career was launched. *Summer and Smoke* (1948), *The Rose Tattoo* (1951), *Camino Real* (1953) followed rapidly, and *Cat on a Hot Tin Roof* in 1958 won still another New York Critics Circle award. Williams' plays appeared rapidly in the late 1950's and early 1960's—*Orpheus Descending* in 1957, *Garden District* and *Suddenly Last Summer* in 1958, and he won still another Critics Circle prize, a fourth, for *Night of the Iguana* in 1961. The 1960's saw the beginnings of a decline, the 1970's real decline —*The Milk Train Doesn't Stop Here Anymore* (1962, 1963), *Slapstick Tragedy* (1966), *Kingdom of Earth* (1968), *In the Bar of a Tokyo Hotel* (1969). Williams became distraught after the death of his long-time friend Frank Merlo in 1963, converted to Roman Catholicism in 1969, was plagued by increasingly serious emotional problems, openly admitted his homosexuality, and suffered a nervous collapse that took him to a St. Louis hospital in 1969. It was ten years before he had some success with *Small Craft Warnings* in 1972. But the 1970's were years of revisions, rewrites, essentially a period of despondency. He published his *Memoirs* in 1975 and died in 1982.

Choosing particular Williams plays for specific discussion in a lecture on tragedy is difficult although our choice of *The Glass Menagerie* and *A Streetcar Named Desire* can hardly be called arbitrary. Along with *Cat on a Hot Tin Roof,* these are the plays most often anthologized, most often discussed in connection with Williams' career, the American theater generally, the idea of American tragedy. Both plays are, of course, firmly entrenched in what has now become for us a truism about modern tragedy, its retreat from great heroes, mythologies, epic struggles and its preoccupation from the time of Ibsen and Strindberg with the ordinary lives—at least ordinary by comparison with Oedipus, Hamlet—of real men and women caught by societal or by personal and psychological struggles and attempting to find meaning and some kind of fulfillment or peace within those struggles. As we have proceeded with American tragedy, even the ordinariness of Ibsen characters seems strong by comparison with the fragile spirits, the lovers of illusion, the trapped dreamers of O'Neill and Miller. With Williams this weakness seems central; in Laura, Blanche, Amanda we find lost souls wounded by life. We wonder again whether "pathetic" seems a better description of the plays than "tragic." But they are real people as conceived by Williams, not allegorical wraiths, not psychological case histories or embodiments of a theme, and they are—especially in *The Glass Menagerie*—seen against larger backdrops.

The world of *The Glass Menagerie* is very much a Williams world—a dingy St. Louis-like apartment entered by a fire-escape. The inhabitants are a domineering, illusion-ridden mother Amanda, abandoned by a soldier-husband whose smiling face in a picture dominates the living room "as if to say, 'I will be smiling forever'"; Laura, a physical—and emotional—cripple afraid to leave the house, content to play the victrola and to indulge her fantasies in the world of her glass menagerie with its glass curios, especially the unicorn; and Tom—so clearly Williams' vision of himself—the disappointing son with dreams like those of his father, but without the courage to escape, chained to live in this claustrophobic world and to work in a local shoe factory, living on movies and dreams. Surrounding this seemingly closed world is the larger arena of life; references to Franco and the Spanish Civil War, to Berchtesgaden, to Neville Chamberlain, to Dizzy Dean of the St. Louis Cardinals, to the Century of Progress, to the labor disturbances of the 1930's, to the Great War enveloping the world interrupt the reveries and dreams of the Wingfields. Yet for all the realism this is essentially a "memory play," as Williams' stage directions indicate, an expressionistic play utilizing stage technique— lighting, scenery, props. As Tom, playing his own stage director, puts it in his opening speech: "Yes, I have tricks in my pocket, I have things up my sleeve. But I am the opposite of a stage magician. He gives you illusion that has the appearance of truth. I give you truth in the pleasant disguise of illusion."

The plot is in many ways simple. Amanda maintains a household, living on memories—real or fancied—of her Blue Mountain Days, days when she was the toast of gentlemen callers, not the trapped housewife of today. Tom is his father's son, a dreamer working in a shoe factory, living at home only for lack of a better place, and a constant source of irritation to his mother. He lacks table manners, smokes too much, reads too much D.H. Lawrence. "I don't want to hear any more," says Tom to Amanda's: Why does Tom go to the movies, stay after midnight, return late, and mope on his job all the next day after three hours sleep, jeopardizing the family's security? Tom's grand outburst sums up his gathering anger and frustration and stuns Amanda:

> Listen! You think I'm crazy about the warehouse? You think I'm in love with the Continental Shoemakers? . . . Every time you come in yelling that God damn *'Rise and Shine!'* 'Rise and Shine!'' I say to myself, 'How *lucky dead* people are!' But I get up! I *go*! For sixty-five dollars a month I give up all that I dream of doing and *being* ever!

Off to the movies again, to his mother's rebukes. Moving towards her, he shouts "I'm going to opium dens! Yes, opium dens, dens of vice and criminals' hangouts, Mother . . . They're going to blow us all skyhigh some night! I'll be glad, very happy, and so will you! You go up, on a broomstick, over Blue Mountain with seventeen gentlemen callers! You ugly—

106

babbling old—*witch.*" Laura retreats to her menagerie, and Amanda, humiliated, demands an apology.

After the outburst, Tom returns from the movies, speaking with Laura, apologizing with great tenderness to his mother and trying desperately to explain why he goes to the movies—"I go to the movies because—I like adventure. Adventure is something I don't have much of at work, so I go to the movies." To his mother's advice that many young men find adventure in their careers, Tom speaks of working in a warehouse: "Man is by instinct a lover, a hunter, a fighter, and none of those instincts are given much play at the warehouse." A truce of sorts is reached by mother and son, as she proposes what is really on her mind, a gentleman caller for Laura. Laura has already disappointed her mother by enrolling in the Rubican Secretarial School and then failing to attend classes because of fear of facing the challenge of school and other people.

Tom has already introduced us to the Gentleman Caller in his opening directorial speech: "He is the most realistic character in the play, being an emissary from a world of reality that we were somehow set apart from." He "is the long delayed but always expected something that we live for." He is Jim O'Connor, a fellow-worker of Tom, a high school classmate of Laura—a breath of reality, handsome, athletic, open, friendly, honest— but engaged to be married. After Amanda's pleadings, Tom invites him to dinner; he and Laura share old memories; Laura is lifted; she hopes, dreams. Jim tells her of her attractiveness, her worth, and for a moment she is happy. They dance; he bumps into her glass menagerie table, and the unicorn loses its horn. They kiss—he encourages her to socialize more—and then the fatal gong of reality is heard, the fatal words: "Laura, I've been going steady!"—"I go out all of the time with a girl named Betty. She's a home-girl like you, and Catholic, and Irish, and in a great many ways we get along fine."—"Being in love has made a new man of me!" "The flower of love is really pretty tremendous!" Desolate, Laura offers Jim the broken unicorn, perhaps a symbol of her broken self. Equally desolate on hearing the news, Amanda—more dreams dashed, "Things have a way of turning out so badly"—berates Tom for his unknowing invitation. Go to the movies, she says. "Go, then! Then go to the moon—you selfish dreamer!"

We are left with Tom—alone on the fire escape, elaborate stage directions indicating that Tom's final words are played against an interior pantomime—with an ennobled Amanda confronting a grateful daughter, glancing at the father's picture, and blowing out the candles. Tom tells us, "I didn't go to the moon, I went much further—for time is the longest distance between two places"—"I left Saint Louis. I descended the steps of this fire-escape for a last time and followed, from then on, in my father's footsteps, attempting to find in motion what was lost in space." He is free, "but I was pursued by something"—"a familiar bit of music," "only a piece of transparent glass."

> Then all at once my sister touches my shoulder. I turn around and look into her eyes . . . . Oh Laura, Laura, I tried to leave you behind, but I am more faithful than I intended to be!
>
> I reach for a cigarette, I cross the street, I run into the movies or a bar, I buy a drink, I speak to the nearest stranger—anything that can blow your candles out! [Laura bends over the candles.]—for nowadays the world is lit by lightning! Blow out your candles, Laura, and so good bye
> . . .

Where, then, lies the tragedy? Is Tom the Ishmael who survives to record the hopelessness, the catastrophe? Roger Stein is harsh in his reading of the play's ending: "The bleakness of William's vision in *The Glass Menagerie* is complete. If Tom is released finally, it is in the words of Job, 'And I only am escaped alone to tell thee.' It is as the author's surrogate, as writer and chronicler of catastrophe, that he emerges at the end."[7] Or does Tom on the one hand record the frailty and illusionism of the mother and sister giving them what the stage directions call a tragic dignity and move on to a deeper awareness, an awareness always tinged with the sense of the tragedy of life?

The world of reality seems even less vivid in *A Streetcar Named Desire* produced two years later. Again the simplest of plot lines hides the deepest kind of tragic vision. Here we have Blanche Dubois returning to her sister Stella's and brother-in-law Stanley Kowalski's home in New Orleans, in—ironically enough—Elysian Fields street, the street of dreams, hopes,

Paradise. Delicate in form and bearing, elegantly dressed "in a white suit with a fluffy bodice, necklace and earrings of pearl, white gloves and hat, looking as if she were arriving at a summer tea or cocktail party in the garden district," she has arrived on "a street-car named Desire." She is a school-teacher from Belle-Reve—how wonderful the names in the play are—resident of a Mississippi white-columned plantation house. She seems the epitome of fine manners as she asks for her sister's residence, finds she is not at home. On the other hand, there are strange rumblings as she enters the apartment, drinks half a tumbler of whiskey, and murmurs to herself: "I've got to get hold of myself!"

Stella returns, and the tragedy slowly develops. Stella, a wonderfully real, open young woman happily married to an earthy, boisterous man, seems satisfied with her life, with a cluttered, crowded apartment. Blanche, increasingly tense, nervous, reaching for more liquor to bolster her spirit, reveals that she has not been fired or resigned, but rather "was so exhausted by all I'd been through my—nerves broke . . . . I was on the verge of lunacy, almost! So Mr. Graves—Mr. Graves is the high school superintendent—he suggested I take a leave of absence." She is clearly unhappy with Stella's life, with her marriage to a 'Polish'—"something like Irish, aren't they?", with New Orleans, with her living arrangements.

Slowly the real story of Blanche unfolds as she talks with Stella, her outward elegance masking a tormented psyche. Yes, death has come to the family; Belle Reve has been lost. "Which of them left a cent of insurance even? Only poor Jesse—one hundred to pay for her coffin. That was all, Stella! And I with my pitiful salary at the school. Yes, accuse me! Sit there and stare at me, thinking I let the place go! I let the place go? Where were you? In bed with your—Polack!"

Enter Stanley, all earth—physical, loud, aggressive, unpretentious—with his friends Steve and Mitch. Earth meets spirit as he encounters Blanche. She flirts a bit; he talks of his lack of refinement and education, inquires about her marriage, evoking from her an ominous, "The boy—the boy died . . . I'm afraid I'm going to be sick." Blanche is attracted to Mitch—Harold Mitchell—of all Stanley's friends; he seems "superior to the others" and a new hope for her. But Stanley, citing the Napoleonic code, presses Blanche on the loss of Belle Reve, on her expensive clothing, digging deep for her secrets.

Blanche's dreams continue; she and Stella will open a dress shop; she will contact an old boy friend to finance the business, but she doesn't even have the money to pay for the telegram. Something must be done about Stella's life, about her baffling—for Blanche—marriage to Stanley. "I am not being or feeling at all superior, Stella. Believe me I'm not! It's just this. This is how I look at it. A man like that is someone to go out with—once—twice—three times when the devil is in you. But live with? Have a child by?" For Blanche, "There is something downright—*bestial*—about him!" Stanley is "a survivor of the stone age! . . . *God*! Maybe we are a long way from being made in God's image, but Stella—my sister—there has been *some* progress since then! Such things as art—poetry and music—such kinds of new light have come into the world since then! In some kinds of people some tenderer feelings have had some little beginning!" Blanche enters a final plea to Stella: *"Don't—don't hang out back with the brutes!"*

Slowly rumors of Blanche's life back home at Laurel gather; Stanley has been pursuing his prey. Blanche and Mitch fall in love, huddling together in their loneliness, searching for a love to give meaning to their lives. They share their deepest secrets, Mitch of his lonely life with his mother, Blanche of her discovery of the homosexuality of the boy she loved at sixteen and of her guilt at his suicide: "It was because—on the dance-floor—unable to stop myself—I'd suddenly said—'I saw! I know! You disgust me . . .'" Mitch and Blanche kiss and embrace, and their hopes soar as Blanche says, "Sometimes—there's God—so quickly!"

The play darkens with Stanley's revelation of the real Blanche of the Flamingo Hotel in Laurel, the belle of the local army camp, finally fired from her school: "They kicked her out of that high school before the spring term ended—and I hate to tell you the reason that step was taken! A seventeen-year-old boy—she'd gotten mixed up with." The forever bathing Blanche sings "Paper Moon"—"It's a Barnum and Bailey world. Just as phony as it can be"—as a backdrop to Stanley's revelation. Stanley has told Mitch the story of Blanche so that he doesn't appear at the birthday party Stella has organized for Blanche. Blanche, cut off from Mitch, given a bus-ticket by Stanley, is tragically alone. Alone, Stella at the hospital to deliver her baby, drinking to drown her sorrows, she is visited by Mitch who confronts her with the story of her past. It is a powerful scene, a scene observed so often in classical and modern tragedy, a scene of confrontation in which there is a coming-to-terms with reality. In a response summing up her life and the life of so many Williams characters, she tells Mitch—"I don't want realism. I want magic! . . . Yes, yes, magic! I try to give that to people. I misrepresent things to them. I don't tell truth. I tell what ought to be truth. And if that is sinful, then let me be damned for it!" She is fit for sex, but not marriage, says Mitch, and in a moment of revelation she speaks of all the "intimacies with strangers was all I seemed able to fill my empty heart with," her last hope now lost with Mitch. Mitch leaves, driven away by her shrieks of "Fire! Fire! Fire!"

Ophelia-like, packed to leave the next day, decked out in evening gown and tiara, she remains alone in the apartment until Stanley's return. Badinage, innuendo, accusations of Stanley's revelations about her, they parry. Menacing forms appear on the walls about a fantasizing Blanche, strange sounds, a frantic, deluded call to Shep Huntleigh of Dallas, and the final encounter with Stanley. "Tiger—tiger! Drop the bottle top! Drop it! We've had this date with each other from the beginning," gloats Stanley, the ravisher-Earth.

Some weeks pass, and Stella, with new life in the house, has resolved to send Blanche away, especially after the story of the Stanley episode which she simply cannot believe. Blanche is a broken figure, as she leaves for the state institution with doctor and matron, "I can smell the sea air. The rest of my time I'm going to spend on the sea. And when I die, I'm going to die on the sea," be buried in "an ocean as blue as . . . my first lover's eyes." She is taken away, Stella tormented by the decision, a sobbing Mitch trying to reach her. And all is quiet—no more struggle. Blanche Dubois extends her hands to the doctor—"Whoever you are—I have always depended on the kindness of strangers."

Again, Williams confronts us with the defeat of dream, the tragedy of the weak in life, the struggle for meaning by the meek of the earth. These men and women—the Wingfields, Blanche,

Shannon, Brick—however frail and pitiful, seem to haunt us, remind us of human weakness. And in that reminder of tragedy, of Williams' deep concern, we are not consoled necessarily, but reminded of the delicate balance of human life, of how so many fail to maintain that balance. Their struggle is not Antigone's or Lear's or even Nora's, but it is a human struggle nevertheless, one ending in isolation, loneliness, and death. And we sit in the theater and see still other representatives of our mortality.

NOTES

1. In *Arthur Miller: A Collection of Critical Essays,* ed. Robert W. Corrigan (Englewood Cliffs, New Jersey: Prentice Hall, Inc., 1969), p. 92.

2. Quotations are from Arthur Miller, *Death of a Salesman* (New York: The Viking Press, 1949).

3. In Corrigan, p. 109.

4. *Arthur Miller's Collected Plays,* with an introduction by the author, 2 vols. (New York: The Viking Press, 1960), I, Preface.

5. In *Tennesse Williams: A Collection of Critical Essays,* ed. Stephen S. Stanton (Englewood Cliffs, New Jersey: Prentice Hall, Inc., 1977), p. 17.

6. Quotations from the plays are from *The Glass Menagerie* (New York: New Directions, 1945), and *A Streetcar Named Desire* (New York: New American Library, 1972).

7. In Stanton, p. 42.

CHAPTER 6

Beyond Tragedy: Beckett and "Waiting for Godot"

"We're waiting for Godot"

I T is difficult to end a series like this one. We have been attempting to deal with the persistence of an idea at once both clear and unclear. That idea—or image if it is a better word—concerns the continuing vitality from fifth-century B.C. Athens to the present of certain plays which portray the fall of basically good men or women who are nonetheless either flawed internally by some weakness or trapped by some external force like fate or heredity.

Certainly the impulse toward something like these plays continues after O'Neill, Miller, and Williams, and in both America, Europe, and elsewhere. For a time, especially during the late 1950's and 1960's, there were the plays of Edward Albee—*The Sandbox, Zoo Story, Who's Afraid of Virginia Woolf, Tiny Alice*—with their sharp critiques of the American dream, the need for human communication instead of illusion. Archibald Macleish's rendering of the Book of Job in the life of *J.B.,* a modern successful businessman, offered the story of a seemingly fortunate man who meets disaster which can be mastered only by love. In France the Absurdist plays of Eugene Ionesco—*The Bald Soprano, The Chairs, Rhinoceros,* to name a few—held center-stage for a time, offering a vision of the meaninglessness of it all and the plight of the individual in the midst of it.

Very much active as we speak are Peter Schaffer in England, exploring the psychological roots of tragedy in theatrically spectacular pieces like *Equus* and *Amadeus,* and Athol Fugard in South Africa, dramatizing racial prejudices and oppression in *A Message from Aloes* and *Master Harold and the Boys,* and a stunning new American playwright Marsha Norman, exploring the individual's search for meaning in her *'Night Mother* and *Traveller in the Dark*. And, already mentioned, we have the American playwrights David Rabe and David Mamet taking us into the pits of American culture to show the tragedy at the heart of it.

Yet if we were to choose one playwright whose presence and influence and profundity of vision tower over modern drama, Samuel Beckett would be a good choice. If his plays have become increasingly lean, the settings increasingly spare, the language increasingly absent, the vision is no less powerful, the attempt to grab a hold on the entire human situation no less poignant.[1] The challenge of dealing with Beckett as writer of tragedy is still with us. As in Sophocles or Shakespeare, the settings are cosmic. The universe seems his arena; human beings, however comic, pathetic, grotesque, his deepest concern. A recent Benedict Nightingale article in the February 26, 1984 *New York Times*—the occasion being Billy Whitelaw's performance in Beckett's *Footfalls* and *Rockaby*—seems unqualified in its emphasis on the universality and importance of Beckett.

> Beckett, alone of contemporary dramatists, continues to keep us mindful of the big, brain-splintering questions. Moreover he does so with a care, love, and unaffected dignity that, paradoxically, seem almost to amount to the human value he denies. And if this fundamental vision has not changed, still less mellowed, its expression has surely reached its apotheosis . . . Again and again he has taken someone's story, a different one each time, and concentrated it, not just to the bone, but to the marrow of the marrow. A line can imply a life in "Footfalls," a word a world in "Rockaby." Seeing the best of Beckett's later work is like opening a door a crack, and finding a universe bleakly unfurled beyond.

Yet there is sharp disagreement with a view like Nightingale's. Jay Carr, in a superb *Boston Globe* article of March 4, 1984, bemoans the fact that "Tragedy doesn't fit us— we've become too small," arguing that "Samuel Beckett, who circles tragedy and approaches it through farce, puts in the mouth of his existential tramps the terminal exhalations of

European culture." A wide range of views on Beckett indeed, and a final challenge to students attempting to see a continuity in the genre of tragedy.

Samuel Beckett was born near Dublin, Ireland on April 13, 1906, to an affluent Protestant family. After graduating from Trinity College where he specialized in French and Italian and performed brilliantly, he taught at the Ecole Normale Supérieure in Paris from 1928 to 1930—he met James Joyce and became part of that legendary circle of artists—and started his career as a writer. He returned to lecture at Trinity and received his M.A. in 1931, writing a study of Proust. He settled permanently in France in 1938, and led a life of great activity, abandoning formal academic work, devoting himself to his writing, travelling all over Europe, fighting for the Resistance in France during World War II. A successful novelist, he began to write plays after the War, and he is now living and active in Paris.

We choose *Waiting for Godot* as our center of attention, not simply because it is perhaps his most famous play, but because it is his fullest and most representative.[2] The others—including *Endgame, Happy Days, Act Without Words I and II, Krapp's Last Tape, Footfalls,* and *Rockaby*, briefer, more silent—intensify through their sheer theatricality the several motifs of *Godot.* Beckett himself calls *Godot* a tragicomedy, and we are puzzled, knowing the history of that genre from the Renaissance to today, by his use of the term. Ruby Cohn's perceptive remarks shed a great deal of light on the problem—"In Godot's continued absence, man becomes a king of shreds and patches, of blindness and dumbness, fit only to play the clown and feed the worms, 'with neither decency nor discretion.' Fallen too low to be a subject for 'right Tragedy,' feeling too much anguish to be capable of 'right Comedy,' Beckett's man, while waiting for Godot, plays a part in a tragicomedy—a part of slapstick-victim in a world that he did not make, and that resists his efforts to make sense of it."[3] *Endgame* utilizes every conceivable trick, pantomime, disguise to play off the bleakest vision of life, the impossible search for human dignity. *Happy Days* shows Winnie, the central character, buried up to her waist in the first act, still able to move her arms and use some of her simple earthly possessions. In the second act we see her buried up to her neck, able to move only her eyes and to see the one other character in the play, Willie, the one source of her "happy days." Krapp listens to the tape recording of his earlier days in his age, and we sense his bitterness and frustration. Yes, comedy, as Cohn argues, does describe in part the situation of the characters; it startles us, makes us laugh while we understand and feel their anguish.

Godot has the ring of what many would call Absurdist tragedy. No plot line could be simpler; no play more cryptic, baffling. A play of two closely connected acts, it is set on two successive evenings on a country road with only a bare tree in sight. Two clownish characters—Chaplinesque is the favorite word used to describe them—appear. Estragon—Gogo is his nickname—who seems of the earth, is emotional, spontaneous as he sits trying to get his boot off, and gives up again with a frustrated "Nothing to be done." Vladamir—nickname Didi—a more proper man, a bit of a thinker, seems concerned about Estragon, would feed him turnips and carrots, but, more important, would minister to his frustration. Pestered by fleas, he examines his bowler, says, "I'm beginning to come round to that opinion. All my life, I've tried to put it from me, saying, Vladamir, be reasonable, you haven't yet tried anything. And so I resumed the struggle." There is a strange kinship between the two, a kinship of poverty and need. Vladamir wants to embrace Estragon.

As Gogo finally removes his boot and airs his smelly feet, Didi becomes quite philosophical about their plight. He introduces the biblical story of how one of the two thieves on Calvary was saved for repenting, and wonders why, since Luke was the only one of the Evangelists to mention the episode, anyone should give it credence. Gogo is puzzled by Didi's use of the expression "Our Saviour," but has no concern for Scriptural topics. As far as he is concerned, people are ignorant apes.

After the initial banter, the title of the play becomes clear or relatively clear. The impulsive Gogo wants to go, to move on; the thoughtful Didi reminds him, "We're waiting for Godot," according to an agreement, by a willow tree, now apparently dead. They must wait, but Estragon wonders why. Banter, often angry exchanges continue, intermingled with that strange sense of camaraderie, even love. "Give me your hand . . . Embrace

116

me!" says Gogo. He proposes hanging immediately, but the prospect of loneliness is too grim. "Don't let's do anything. It's safer," he says.

Enter Pozzo and Lucky, mysterious characters so often—and perhaps wisely—described in terms of master and slave, Pozzo with whip driving Lucky with a long rope around his neck, Lucky carrying a heavy bag, folding stool, picnic basket with chicken and wine, a greatcoat. We are struck by the nature of this relationship just as we were by the tenderness of Vladamir and Estragon. Didi and Gogo seem like Lear's "unaccommodated man," stripped to the bare essentials of their humanity, but still enduring, talking. Pozzo and Lucky are burdened with things, never really communicating with one another. As the pairs of humanity examine each other, Pozzo proclaims, "You are human beings nonetheless," although he knows nothing of the Godot they are awaiting. Estragon feeds himself with the chicken bones left by a gorging Pozzo and a silent, battered Lucky. Vladamir, ever the thoughtful observer, comments, "It's a scandal!—"To treat a man . . . like that . . . I think that . . . no . . . a human being . . . a human being . . . no . . . it's a scandal."

Hugh Kenner's analysis of this first-act contrast of the two pairs is most penetrating:

> If these two, master and servant, epitomize the busy world from which Didi and Gogo have seceded, there is no record of the act of secession. Rather the contrasting pairs appear to epitomize not so much ways of life so much as modes of being. Amid the great void which they strive to fill up with exercises and conversation, Didi and Gogo circulate about one another with delectable affection . . . Lucky and Pozzo live with their heads, these two moving hither and thither, Pozzo . . . imposing with his campstool and ceremonial a prissy elegance on their halts; Lucky, treacherous, miserable . . . and dancing or thinking on command. There is no love here, and the play's waiting seems incontestably preferable to its journeying.[4]

There is at times in the first act a touch of lost tenderness in Pozzo. To Vladamir he says, "The tears of the world are a constant quantity. For each one who begins to weep somewhere else another stops." As night falls, he speaks to Didi and Gogo,

117

". . . but behind this veil of gentleness and peace night is charging and will burst upon us pop! like that just when we least expect it. That's how it is on this bitch of an earth." In the midst of this gathering, the hitherto silent Lucky is prodded and prodded until he delivers his fantastic, non-stop speech, a brilliant Beckett parody of all philosophical reasoning and thought until he is stopped, his thinking hat removed, and returned to his servile state. Pozzo and Lucky move on, but Didi and Gogo must wait for Godot. A boy enters with a message from Godot that he will not come tonight but certainly tomorrow. Under moonlight Didi and Gogo reminisce about their years together. In rapid succession they consider separating, decide against it; plan to go, but, as the first act ends, they do not move. They are fixed in their waiting.

Act II, as already noted, seems to offer more of the same. There is a willow leaf on the previously barren tree. Vladamir with hat and Estragon with boot parry with one another, finally embrace, and stay together. Vladamir reconstructs the meeting with Pozzo and Lucky to a forgetful Estragon, and for a time communication almost seems to break down. They play at Pozzo and Lucky, slave and master, make up still again, and ask for God's pity.

Pozzo and Lucky appear again, but how differently—one blind and the other dumb—and they plead for help. Eloquently Vladamir feels their need, that strangely all mankind and its plight is somehow embodied on this plain. It is a post-atomic, futuristic setting that is evoked by his touching words, something beyond even Matthew Arnold's "darkling plain" and "ignorant armies" and their "clash by night." "But at this place, at this moment of time, all mankind is us, whether we like it or not. Let us make the most of it before it is too late." Earlier Hamlet had seen "To be or not to be" as the central question of his tragic world. Vladamir is persuaded that his is a different question, "What are we doing here?" Further, and we wonder as modern readers how we are to take him, "we are blessed," says Vladamir, "that we happen to know the answer. Yes, in this immense confusion one thing alone is clear. We are waiting for Godot to come . . . ." The incredulous, earthy Estragon cries, "We are all born mad. Some remain so."

Didi and Gogo minister to Lucky and Pozzo, listen to Pozzo's biblical sounding, "They give birth astride of a grave, the light gleams an instant, then it's night once more." Vladamir and Estragon struggle to understand. Was Pozzo Godot? Do I wake or sleep, wonders Vladamir? Will you help me to take off my boots, asks Estragon? With great tenderness toward Gogo who has fallen asleep, Didi questions what has happened: "That with Estragon my friend, at this place, until the fall of night, I waited for Godot? That Pozzo passed with his carrier, and that he spoke to us?" But what do these things mean? Didi, in the tradition of tragic questioners although hardly appearing like them, wonders. Who is he? What is he doing? What does his existence mean? Are men no more than this? Estragon, sharing the same predicament, will not think very deeply. In another tradition of tragic survivors, he is concerned about his physical endurance. As Vladamir reflects on a sleeping Estragon, "He'll tell me about the blows he received and I'll give him a carrot." Vladamir wonders whether he can go on.

Henderson Forsythe as Vladamir speaks to "a boy" in Beckett's *Waiting for Godot*.

In the midst of this moving scene, the boy returns, or is it another boy-servant of Godot? Vladamir questions and finds that this new boy is the brother of yesterday's visitor, a boy who tends sheep, not goats. Godot will come tomorrow, he assures Didi and Gogo. The moon rises as the two stand alone. Gogo proposes hanging themselves, but with what? A rope, of course, but they have none. With Gogo's belt perhaps, but it's too short. There will be time and opportunity tomorrow, they procrastinate. "I can't go on like this," cries Gogo only to hear Didi's stoical, "That's what you think." Gogo proposes parting as a relief, but Vladamir matches the strategy of hanging themselves tomorrow unless Godot comes.

Estragon pulls up his trousers; Vladamir suggests leaving the place of watching and waiting. They both, however, stand still and do not move. As Didi and Gogo stand fast at the end of the play, do not move in spite of their resolutions to the contrary, we have, it seems, something of Beckett's essential vision. It is not one of questions answered or of evils righted or of suffering man rewarded. Neither was this the vision of Sophocles and Shakespeare with their dead Antigone and Hamlet, their blinded Oedipus; nor was it the vision of Ibsen with his resolute Nora Helmer facing the darkness outside the doll's house. The inmates of Harry Hope's bar, of the Tyrone household, Willy Loman dying for a dream, Tom Wingfield and Blanche Dubois trapped in dreams—none of these offers facile solutions to the questions of O'Neill, Miller, Williams. Beckett, of course, carries us to the ultimate bleakness, a scene beyond even the storm-ravaged plain of *King Lear*. Unaccommodated man is no more than Vladamir and Estragon in his vision, humanity stripped of everything in a cosmic wilderness, stripped of everything except the capacity to love, to endure, to wait.

NOTES

1. For a perceptive and illuminating treatment of narrative and dramatic technique in Beckett, see Kristin Morrison, *Canters and Chronicles: The Use of Narrative in the Plays of Samuel Beckett and Harold Pinter* (Chicago and London: The University of Chicago Press, 1983).

2. Quotations are from *Waiting for Godot* (New York: Grove Press, Inc., 1954).

3. *Samuel Beckett: The Comic Gamut* (New Brunswick, New Jersey: Rutgers University Press, 1962), p. 225.

4. *Samuel Beckett: A Critical Study* (Berkeley: University of California Press, 1973), pp. 154-155.

Epilogue

IN our end is our beginning. As we ranged widely in these six lectures—perhaps too widely—over great drama in ancient Greece, Renaissance England, nineteenth and twentieth-century Europe and America, we have, of course, admired the dramatic achievement of Sophocles, Shakespeare, Ibsen, O'Neill, Miller, Williams, and Beckett. These are certainly major playwrights by any artistic standard. Yet our concern has been more focussed, our questions more particular. We have wondered about the persistence of a kind of drama that has come to be called tragedy in both academic and popular discussion. On the one hand, we found enormous diversity in the societies, settings, characters, problems, and language in these dramatic worlds. On the other, we have found certain common patterns that tempt us to see links among the plays and the heroes and heroines. We have been somewhat arbitrary—some would say even capricious—in using a particular group of writers. Certainly there are other great playwrights who should be included. We have been similarly arbitrary in using Oedipus, Antigone, King Lear, Nora Helmer, Hedda Gabler, the Alvings, the lonely inhabitants of Harry Hope's bar, the doomed Tyrone family, Willy Loman, the Wingfields, Blanche Dubois, Vladamir and Estragon as characters who seemed fertile subjects for exploring our concerns and questions. Many of those attending these lectures might quite rightly feel that important heroes and heroines have been neglected. But six lectures, as we suggested at the outset, are too few, and they bring opportunities and dangers, both of which are obvious to those who have had ears to hear and eyes to read.

Yet the opportunities have been rich. We have, of course, found no magic definition of tragedy although we have not hidden our prejudices in exploring a possible model. That model envisages a man or woman of importance—importance measured not only by rank or honor, but by a certain largeness of spirit. It envisages that man or woman, fated or flawed or both, meeting death or disaster, a death or disaster often striking us as undeserved, unjust. It further reveals these central characters as struggling with their fate, their situation, struggling to find some kind of meaning even when the meaning is elusive, even when the struggle varies from crying out to some divine power to seeking escape in a St. Louis movie house to waiting for something to happen in the midst of an existential loneliness. Our model has explored finally our involvement as audiences in the plight of these men and women, our sense that all is not lost even when it appears to be. We find a moment of calm after the storm, admiration after pity and fear, identification with fellow humans after puzzlement with characters who seem remote from us. It is perhaps too large and general a paradigm—and we have seen sharp critical disagreement with it—but it has provided us at the very least with the chance to marvel at the genius of the dramatists and to advance our own thinking about what we have called the persistence of tragedy. If these lectures have provided that chance to marvel and to do our own thinking, they have served a useful purpose.

Some years ago in an extraordinary paragraph in a graduate school course paper, my former student James Walker caught succinctly and perceptively something that has continued to impress me about this persisting tragic spirit. I should like to close with that paragraph:

> We all move, regardless of personal differences towards these ends [love, success, meaning]. The substance of tragedy are those events, sometimes caused by ignorance, sometimes simply by chance, which sometimes halt this movement. The significance of this event is magnified when the subject is a figure so great in spirit that he commands our respect, compels our emotions, and so involves our psyche that his folly, his suffering becomes our own. In experienceing this, we are forced to question our own illusions, our own possibilities, and ultimately the essence of what we believe we are. And sometimes through all of this, we find wisdom and humility, and at the same time an exhilarating appreciation for the fragile, yet wondrously brave, creature that we are. This is the essence of tragedy.

124

Selected Bibliography

In addition to materials listed in footnotes, readers should find the following selected bibliography helpful as they pursue reading in tragedy.

GENERAL

Brooks, Cleanth, ed. *Tragic Themes in Western Literature.* New Haven: Yale University Press, 1955.

Butcher, S.H. *Aristotle's Theory of Poetry and Fine Arts,* 4th ed. London: Macmillan, 1932.

Corrigan, Robert W., ed. *Tragedy: A Critical Anthology.* Boston: Houghton Mifflin, 1971.

Frye, Northrop. *The Anatomy of Criticism.* Princeton, New Jersey: Princeton University Press, 1971.

Hegel, Wilhelm Friedrich. *The Philosophy of Fine Art,* tr. F.P.B. Osmaston. London: Bell, 1920.

Jaspers, Karl. *Tragedy Is Not Enough.* Boston: Beacon Press, 1952.

Krieger, Murray. *The Tragic Vision.* New York: Holt, Rinehart, and Winston, 1960.

Krutch, Joseph Wood. *The Modern Temper.* New York: Harcourt Brace and World, 1929.

_____. *A Krutch Omnibus: Forty Years of Social and Literary Criticism.* New York: William Morrow, 1970.

Levin, Richard. *Tragedy: Plays, Theory, Criticism.* New York: Harcourt Brace and World, 1960.

Lucas, F.L. *Tragedy in Relation to Aristotle's Poetics.* New York: Harcourt Brace, 1928.

Nietzsche, Friedrich. *The Birth of Tragedy and the Genealogy of Morals.* tr. Francis Golffing. Garden City, New York: Doubleday and Company, 1956.

Roberts, Patrick. *The Psychology of Tragic Drama.* London and Boston: Routledge and Kegan Paul, 1975.

Schwarz, Alfred. *From Buchner to Beckett: Dramatic Theory and the Modes of Tragic Drama.* Athens, Ohio: Ohio University Press, 1978.

Scott, Nathan, ed. *The Tragic Vision and the Christian Faith.* New York: Modern Language Association, 1957.

Sewall, Richard. *The Vision of Tragedy.* New Edition, Enlarged. New Haven and London: Yale University Press, 1980.

Weisinger, Herbert. *Tragedy and the Paradox of the Fortunate Fall.* East Lansing, Michigan: State College Press, 1953.

Williams, Raymond. *Modern Tragedy.* Stanford, California: Stanford University Press, 1966.

GREEK TRAGEDY

Bowra, C.M. *Sophoclean Tragedy.* Oxford: Clarendon Press, 1944.

_____. *The Greek Experience.* Cleveland: World Publishing, 1958.

Greene, William C. *Moira: Fate, Good, and Evil in Greek Thought.* Cambridge, Mass.: Harvard University Press, 1944.

Knox, Bernard. *Oedipus at Thebes.* New Haven: Yale University Press, 1957.

Murray, Gilbert Murray. *Five Stages of Greek Religion.* Garden City, New York: Doubleday, 1955.

Wheelwright, Philip. *The Burning Fountain.* Bloomington: Indiana University Press, 1968.

Wilson, Edmund. *The Wound and the Bow.* Boston: Houghton Mifflin, 1941.

SHAKESPEARE

Bevington, David, ed. *Twentieth Century Interpretations of "Hamlet."* Englewood Cliffs, New Jersey: Prentice-Hall, 1968.

Bradley, A.C. *Shakespearean Tragedy.* New York: Meridian, 1955.

Brower, R.A. *Hero and Saint: Shakespeare and the Greco-Roman Heroic Tradition.* Oxford: Clarendon Press, 1971.

Bush, Douglas. *The Renaissance and Christian Humanism.* Toronto: University of Toronto Press, 1939.

Campbell, Lily B. *Shakespeare's Tragic Heroes.* Cambridge University Press, 1930.

Cunningham, J.V. *Woe or Wonder: The Emotional Effect of Shakespearean Tragedy.* Denver: University of Denver Press, 1951.

Elton, William R. *King Lear and the Gods.* San Marino, California: Huntington Library, 1966.

Fraser, Russel. *Shakespeare's Poetics in Relation to "King Lear."* London: Routledge and Paul, 1962.

Frye, Northrop. *Fools of Time: Studies in Shakespearean Tragedy.* Toronto: University of Toronto Press, 1967.

Harbage, Alfred, ed. *Shakespeare: The Tragedies.* Englewood Cliffs, New Jersey: Prentice-Hall, 1964.

Jones, Ernest. *Hamlet and Oedipus.* New York: Norton, 1949.

Leech, Clifford. *Shakespeare's Tragedies.* London: Chatto and Windus, 1950.

Levin, Harry. *The Question of Hamlet.* New York: Viking, 1961.

Mack, Maynard. *"King Lear" in Our Time.* Berkeley: University of California Press, 1965.

Ornstein, Robert. *The Moral Vision of Jacobean Tragedy.* Westport, Conn.: Greenwood, 1975.

Prosser, Eleanor. *Hamlet and Revenge.* Stanford, California: Stanford University Press, 1967.

Raleigh, W., *et al,* eds. *Shakespeare's England: An Account of the Life and Manners of His Age,* 2 vols. Oxford: Clarendon Press, 1916.

Ribner, Irving. *Patterns in Shakespearean Tragedy.* New York: Barnes and Noble, 1960.

Tillyard, E.M.W. *The Elizabethan World Picture.* New York: Random House, 1943.

Wilson, J. Dover. *What Happens in "Hamlet."* New York: Cambridge University Press, 1959.

IBSEN

Bentley, Eric. *The Playwright as Thinker.* New York: Reynall and Hitchcock, 1946.

Beyer, Edvard. *Ibsen: The Man and His Work,* tr. Marie Wells. New York: Taplinger, 1980.

Gilman, Richard. *The Making of Modern Drama.* New York: Farrar, Straus and Giroux, 1974.

Greene, David. *Reality and the Heroic Pattern: Last Plays of Ibsen, Shakespeare, and Sophocles.* Chicago: University of Chicago Press, 1967.

Lyons, Charles. *Henrik Ibsen: The Divided Consciousness.* Carbondale: Southern Illinois University Press, 1972.

Lucas, F.L. *The Drama of Ibsen and Strindberg.* New York: Macmillan, 1962.

Meyer, Michael. *Henrik Ibsen: A Biography.* New York: Doubleday, 1971.

Northan, John. *Ibsen: A Critical Study.* Cambridge: University Press, 1973.

Steiner, George. *The Death of Tragedy.* New York: Knopf, 1961.

Tennant, P.F.D. *Ibsen's Dramatic Technique.* New York: Humanities, 1965.

Webb, E. *The Dark Dove: The Sacred and the Secular in Modern Literature.* Seattle: University of Washington Press, 1975.

O'NEILL

Clark, Barrett H. *Eugene O'Neill: The Man and His Plays.* New York: Dover, 1947.

Engel, Edwin A. *The Haunted Heroes of Eugene O'Neill.* Cambridge, Mass.: Harvard University Press, 1953.

Falk, Doris. *Eugene O'Neill and the Tragic Tension.* New Brunswick, New Jersey: Rutgers University Press, 1958.

Frazer, Winifred D. *Love as Death in "The Iceman Cometh."* Gainesville: University of Florida Press, 1967.

Gelb, Arthur and Barbara. *O'Neill.* New York: Harper's, 1962.

Kinne, Wisner Payne. *George Pierce Baker and the American Theater.* Cambridge, Mass.: Harvard University Press, 1954.

Sheaffer, Louis. *O'Neill: Son and Artist.* Boston: Little, Brown, 1973.

MILLER

Harshburger, Karl. *The Burning Jungle: An Analysis of Arthur Miller's "Death of a Salesman."* Boston: University Press of America, 1980.

Huftel, Sheila. *Arthur Miller: The Burning Glass.* New York: Citadel, 1965.

Nelson, Benjamin. *Arthur Miller: Portrait of a Playwright.* New York: McCoy, 1967.

WILLIAMS

Falk, Signi. *Tennessee Williams.* New York: Twayne, 1962.

Nelson, Benjamin. *Tennessee Williams: The Man and His Work.* New York: I. Obolensky, 1961.

Tischler, Nancy. *Tennessee Williams: Rebellious Puritan.* New York: Citadel, 1961.

BECKETT

Bair, Deirdre. *Samuel Beckett: A Biography.* New York: Harcourt Brace Jovanovich, 1978.

Cohn, Ruby. *Back to Beckett.* Princeton, New Jersey: Princeton University Press, 1973.

Hassan, Ihab. *The Literature of Silence: Henry Miller and Samuel Beckett.* Magnolia, Mass.: Peter Smith, 1967.

Hesla, David. *The Shape of Chaos: An Interpretation of the Art of Samuel Beckett.* Minnesota: University of Minnesota Press, 1971.

Kenner, Hugh. *Samuel Beckett.* Berkeley: University of California Press, 1968.

Mercer, Vivian. *Beckett/Beckett.* New York: Oxford University Press, 1977.